Where the PEACE of God Reigns!

Mike and Cher Goldbloom

WHERE THE PEACE OF GOD REIGNS

Pastor Mike and Cher Goldbloom

Shalom Assembly of God
1862 Kimball Avenue
Willow Grove, PA 19090

ISBN Number: 978-0-9826045-3-3

Printed in the United States of America.

Table of Contents

Dedication

We would like to dedicate this book to our Lord Jesus the Messiah. Without Him these stories would not have taken place. Our hope is that you will be encouraged and strengthened in your faith because Jesus is the true Shalom (peace).

We also want to acknowledge our Family at Shalom Assembly of God, as well as all of those who have stood with us through the years, with a special remembrance to Virgie, for planting the seed of life into my very soul.

Your love, prayers, words of encouragement and financial support has enabled us to proclaim this good news message of hope and eternal life. Thank you so much, and you will forever be in our hearts.

To our children, Rachel, Ben (Rachel's husband), and Sarah. We have seen the Lord's goodness and faithfulness in your lives. We want to leave this "Legacy of Love" with you, and your children, our grand-daughter Charlotte Love, and others yet to be born. We love you.

Foreword

Mike and Cheryl Goldbloom are two of the sweetest people I have ever had the privilege of knowing. Yet more than that, they are both "living miracles" of God's love.

This book you are holding, and soon to read, will not merely arm you with the truth of God's peace, it will demonstrate just how God's peace can flow through your life as it has Mike and Cheryl's lives.

You will grow to love God more as you grow to love this unique couple who share their personal story of God's peace in their lives.

Dr. Joe Van Koevering
Host of International Prophecy Conference
Senior Pastor of Gateway Christian Center

Preface

The Shalom Assembly of God is exactly as it is entitled: A gathering place of peace; when I enter the walls, I do enter His chambers. I can recall once standing in the center of the sanctuary with Pastor Mike, Cheryl, and family with hands joined in prayer. I literally felt the weight of the Lord's presence so heavily and so lovingly embrace us while we prayed. I could also, at that moment, sense the spirit whispering to me, "We were standing in full circle", or the complete and perfect picture of the Bride fully prepared for her Lord.

As the Word says, "Every tribe, tongue, nation, and people, and His kingdom come, (in earth and on earth), as it is in heaven." That day in the center of the sanctuary, in that assembly, I knew I'd entered the true Shalom of God. The Shalom Assembly of God "is" exactly as it "is" entitled!

Kim Sledge Allen
Co-founder of the Paradise Project Ministries
Member of recording group Sister Sledge

Where the Peace of God Reigns

Written for Cher by Mike

The sun was setting, dusk was near,
Another day, unending tears
The moon came up, the stars appeared,
Increasing darkness mixed with fears

Once again, – morning began –
This must be God's wonderful plan
A boy and girl went out to play;
this was no ordinary Summer's Day

The sky was bright, the ocean blue,
This was the day – I first saw you
We talked, we swam, we said good-bye,
In our hearts was placed an invisible tie

Time was spent, I had to go,
Deep inside I knew, I would always know
Two lives became One on that Summer's Day;
My heart would be filled with joy, always

That Summer's Day, That Summer's Day –
When both of us went out to play
My life was changed when I met you;
God was showing us what He wanted to do

That Summer's Day, That Summer's Day –
I didn't know then, He had full sway
Tears of joy now deep within –
The beautiful smell of the summer wind

That Summer's Day, That Summer's Day –
God was at work, while we were at play
His blessing now, came into view –
A Gift from God, it was you …

Introduction

As we share this story of our lives, we have discovered what Jesus said is true. John 16:33 says, "I have told you these things, so that in me you may have peace. In this world you will have trouble. But take heart! I have overcome the world."

In relationships, family, among friends, at work, and even in ministry, every step of the way we have encountered road blocks, spiritual hindrances, detours, and heartache.

Just like you, we have felt the real pain of broken promises and disappointments. We have learned to put our hand in God's hand, and to allow Him to lead us through every chapter of our lives.

One of our foundation scriptures is Proverbs 3:5-6: "Trust in the Lord with all your heart, and lean not on your own understanding; in all your ways acknowledge Him, and He will make your paths straight."

With each new day, even when we can't see the future, we put God first, and invite Him in to intervene, and have watched Him supernaturally lead us into His will for our lives. When our thoughts are racing, and our emotions are volatile, we have seen the Lord fulfill His Word.

In Philippians 4:6-7 it says: "Do not be anxious

about anything, but in everything, by prayer and petition, with thanksgiving, present your requests to God. And the peace of God, which transcends all understanding, will guard your hearts and minds in Christ Jesus."

While you read this book we encourage you to apply the principles of worship, prayer, and the leading of the Holy Spirit to your daily life. As a result, the peace of God will reign in your life as well.

CHAPTER 1
THE MASTER'S PLAN

There Was Something "Pure" About Her ...

On a sunny, summer day, July 18, 1971 our families were both staying at the same motel in Longport, New Jersey. The island at this location is only 1100 feet wide, with the ocean on one side, and the bay on the other. The motel was a two story concrete building with a brick front, where the main office was located. There were two buildings, separated by a parking lot. Its name was Ocean Bay. How appropriate. What a magnificent view of these two bodies of water.

To the east you can see the vastness of the ocean, aligned with the tan colored sand and a mixture of seashells, with crashing waves in the background. To the west you can see the bay which is more serene. The bulkhead was comprised of huge stones where fishermen would cast their lines hoping for a keeper. Looking back, we know it was not a coincidence. Out of all the possibilities and variables, all the hotels, shore towns, and even the timing ... that two individuals ... living in separate geographical locations, from different ethnic and religious backgrounds, would share a new beginning from that day on.

I was a fourteen year old Jewish boy, growing up in Philadelphia, and had just completed my Bar Mitzvah. Cher was thirteen years old, always believed in God and His Son Jesus, but was unaware of being born of His Spirit. Some said it would not work; there are just too many obstacles, especially in our world and the problems that already exist. Others said we were too young, which in most cases is true. But somehow we knew in our early teens and unsettled time of our lives, that this person would someday be the one that we would walk down the aisle with, and marry.

Join me as I recall the day we first met. On the last day of our family vacation, I caught a glimpse of Cher, and knew I wanted to meet her. Knowing time was running out, and wanting to speak with her, I approached Cher's brother and asked him what her name was. Summoning all the courage I had, I called out from the second floor balcony, as she was coming back from the pool area. When our eyes met, we immediately smiled at each other, but did not have the chance to speak yet. I found out later her heart wanted to respond with a hello, but the words were not outwardly expressed. She had a mixture of emotions; feeling a bit timid and not wanting to show too much of an interest at first. I started feeling pressure wondering if I would ever see her again.

My parents had invited another family to come with us, who had two sons my age. Later on that day, as I took a walk with them, we passed the room where

Cher was staying. She could see us as we passed the window, to check out the bay view on the island. She knew something was stirring, and felt very excited. She wanted so badly to talk with me. As the day was passing, and my friends went on their way, Cher and I had our first conversation outside of the motel room, on the second floor balcony, where I first had called out her name. When I first began to talk with her, she seemed more mature and possibly older than me. So I told her I was sixteen, because I was afraid she would think I was too young. I was only fourteen at the time, and discovered that she was thirteen. Later we laughed about it.

We spoke about our love for music. At that time we both played the guitar, and mentioned our favorite bands and musicians. I had just learned to play, and was captivated by the sound of the electric guitar. Rock music was the genre of the day, and I listened to the music more than the words. For my older sister's birthday, my dad took her to see the Beatles at JFK Stadium in Philadelphia, and I tagged along. From that time on, I listened to my sister's records over and over when they were still produced on vinyl. I also tried to play songs from the Rolling Stones, Ten Years After and Chicago. Cher was involved with acting and singing, and played the electric guitar. We were enjoying our conversation and time was going by so quickly.

We decided to swim in the pool together, and I wanted to show her how long I was able to hold my breath under water. I had years of experience starting at an early age in the bathtub, with my mask and snorkel, copying the show Sea Hunt. After all at the age of fourteen what could I do to impress her!! From the pool area, the beach was just steps away, so we decided to take a walk to peek at the beautiful ocean. Being a hot summer day, the sky above us was brilliant blue, as the sun sparkled on top of the waves.

From where we stood the beach is wide, with about a quarter mile of sand to reach the water. No public parking is allowed in Longport, so we had the beach to ourselves. Even till this day I always tell Cher jokingly, that I rented out the beach just for us. We wished we had more time together, but knowing I had to leave soon, and go back to Pennsylvania, I asked Cher for her phone number, and full name. I repeated her last name, just in case I would happen to misplace the piece of paper with her number on it. I had never done this before, and I knew how important that was to me. I couldn't put it into words then, but I now know that God was drawing us together.

Even though our time together was brief, I knew there was something different about her, and deep inside felt one day she would be my wife. According to the message in rock music, you are supposed to look for a girl "wild and free", but there was something "pure" about her. Cher sensed that it was more than just a physical attraction, and felt that I had a deeper insight to who she really was.

That summer I was attending Camp America in Bucks County, Pennsylvania. The bus trip from Philadelphia to camp passed by the street that Cher lived on. During a phone conversation, I asked her if she would stand on the corner and wave to us as we passed by. I wanted to prove to my friends that I really did have a girl-friend. As the bus drove up the hill in this suburban neighborhood, approaching her street, we all were pressing our faces against the window in anticipation of seeing this beauty that I had described. We were almost there, and my heart started racing. There it was – Lenape Drive; and she wasn't there. I'll never forget the sinking feeling in the pit of my stomach when we passed by her street and Cher was a no-show.

Where was she? Was she no longer interested? Did my friends think I was making this all up? After all they heard the whole story. The rest of the bus ride to camp I remained silent, shocked and disappointed. At this early stage in our relationship, my heart was broken. I was unaware that she was not standing me up, but actually was not feeling well, (maybe she was love-sick). This is a perfect illustration of expectations in life that go unfulfilled. On the surface it may look hopeless, but the story is not over. When I called Cher later that evening, she explained, and I realized my fears were unnecessary.

We made plans for our first date to go to Warminster, a town she had lived in for a short time. To get to Cher's house I had to take a train and a cab; then her mom drove us to the intersection of Street Road and York Road and dropped us off. We walked to a place called Grant's, and had French fries and a coke. I experienced that day the first of many of Cher's special cuisine tastes, one of which was eating the fries with black pepper and ketchup. We also walked amongst a field of dandelions, sort of like out of a movie script, where we shared our thoughts and dreams to one another.

We were not old enough to drive, so our meetings were very special. We appreciated every moment. There were times I would take a cab, train, ride my bike and sometimes even hitch-hike, depending on the weather and time of day. Because of our long distance relationship, (or so it seemed), a little over seven miles, it was not easy to see each other. One of our favorite songs at the time was, "So Far Away" by Carole King. It just seemed appropriate and even made us long for those times together even more.

As our relationship continued to grow, (and before we knew the Lord) Cher bought me a Mizpah, which are two halves of a coin with a scripture on it. Genesis 31:49 says: "May the Lord watch between me and thee, while we are absent from one another." We each wore a half around the neck, and it was a reminder of the commitment we had to each other. I bought Cher a mezuzah from the gift shop at the synagogue, which is a constant reminder of God's presence and His commandments. During these early years we didn't talk much about our beliefs, but there was this underlying current that was present and ongoing.

During the days we both were busy with our studies, and had to wait for weekends to see each other. This was before cell phones and e-mails, so we did a lot of talking on the telephone, when it was available. We knew our relationship was growing stronger because during the times of separation, we literally felt sick. I remember the first time I was invited to Cher's dad's house for Sunday dinner. He picked me up at my house in Philly, in a gold Cadillac, (my first limo ride)! No one warned me, and I did not know what to expect at the traditional Sunday night Italian dinner! When we arrived the whole family was there; brothers, grand-parents, dogs, and pig in the oven. The gravy had been cooking all day with the meat, and the smell of garlic hit your nostrils as you walked in the doorway. After being introduced and hearing that my name was Goldbloom, they gasped thinking I could be kosher, and would not be able to eat most of the food prepared. After putting them at ease, we all laughed because my family did not keep the dietary laws.

It's forty years later and they won't let me live down that day, because after the bread, salad, pasta, pig roast, meatballs and sausage, chicken, veggies, and dessert, I was told that it would be an insult if I did not have seconds and thirds. After responding and taking more food each time, (to make a good impression) they kept telling me to Mangia (eat – in Italian).

They still can't believe how much I ate that day. When her dad dropped me off, and I had to say good-bye to Cher; that sad feeling returned. Seeing Cher was the hi-light of my life; and without her there was something missing. We got together as often as possible, and I started to visit Cher during the week after school, and then I would be home for dinner. We used to meet at the Cedarbrook Mall and hang out at the record store, where Cher worked part-time.

On Saturdays we took the C bus from the Ogontz terminal all the way down Broad Street to Center City for Cher's voice lessons. We would then go to different restaurants for lunch, and sometimes see a movie. One of our favorite snacks was at Calico Kitchen where we had black and white milkshakes. Aside from our studies, I was on my high school swim team, which meant that during the week there was practice at the YMCA in Germantown, and work outs in the gym weight room. Cher was involved with her school's play productions, and choir ensemble. Cher always seemed to have a lead role that included having a kiss. It wasn't so much the stage kiss that bothered me, but it was all the practice that was involved. If that wasn't enough, the guys would want to go out with her which made me insecure that I might lose her. She always assured me that it was just a show. We continued to learn more about each other and our early love was blossoming.

But God demonstrates his own love for us in this: While we were still sinners, Christ died for us. – Romans 5:8

The steps of a good man are ordered by the Lord. – Psalm 37:23

God was working behind the scenes, even when we did not recognize it. Praise His Holy Name!

CHAPTER 2

TWO DIFFERENT LIVES – ONE LORD

Confessing Jesus As Messiah ...

Three years had gone by since we first met. I was in my last year both at Central High School and Confirmation Class in the synagogue. Cher was in the 10th grade at a school that had religion as one of her courses, which always sparked an interest of this subject. During these years we were maturing and learning more about each other, with this underlying hunger for spiritual things. We were hearing in the music that we listened to, different religious messages such as, Buddhism, Hinduism, Hare Krishna, and Transcendental Meditation. Since I was interested in karate one of my favorite television shows was Kung-Fu.

I thought it was great that the main character could bring peace and healing to any situation. At that time the world offered many different paths they said would lead to God, but the Lord's hand was always upon us. He kept us away from the cults that were springing up all around.

Cher's mom, Shirley (Oma) was working hard for her family going into homes selling baby portraits. At one of the homes that she had gone to, there was a woman who invited her to church. Do you understand the importance of that conversation? That was another major part of where our lives went from there. Oma had asked us if we would ever want to go visit this church and we said that we would.

Some of the people from the church came to visit at Cher's home, and we remember them sharing the gospel. The next church event was a movie which we attended called "The Thief in the Night." The message shared about the second return of Jesus, and the urgency to be ready. At the end of the service an invitation was given for anyone who would raise their hand to accept Jesus as their personal Savior. I wanted to respond but felt like there was a weight on my shoulder keeping my hand down. I thought about receiving the Lord, but remembered "Jewish people don't believe in Jesus." I knew my family would disapprove. Cher always believed in Jesus and His Word, but did not know there was a personal relationship with Him that she could have.

Knowing ABOUT Him, we found out is different than KNOWING Him. All of this was raising many questions to us, and we wanted to know what did the Bible actually reveal? That night we went to our separate homes, without personally receiving Jesus, but the seed that had been planted in our lives was now being watered. I knew I did not have a relationship with God, and contemplated the consequences of receiving Jesus as my Messiah. Cher never had heard about the scriptures revealing the prophecies of His return, and wondered why.

A week went by, and on Resurrection Sunday, April 14, 1974, we attended a church service for the first time. I was 16 years old, living at home in Philadelphia, having to think of an excuse to explain why I was leaving so early. Cher's family planned to attend also. As was our custom, Cher and I arrived before the service began. Approaching the church driveway on this spring morning, we could see the colonial brick style structure with white columns that stood three stories tall in the front of the edifice. This would be a very special place to us!

When we had seen the movie a week before, we sat in the back of the church. This day we made a bee-line towards the front of the sanctuary, facing a magnificent stained glass window depicting Jesus knocking on the door of our hearts. Sitting on the fourth row, center aisle, we were anticipating every word that would be spoken that day.

The pastor's message was passionate, fiery, and it seemed that he spoke directly to us. He shared the message of hope and life in Jesus. The Gospel presentation was clear. Our sins have separated us from God, and we needed atonement. ("covering" for our sins) Jesus fulfilled all of the Old Testament prophecies concerning the Passover Lamb whose blood was shed so that death and judgment would pass over us.

"Surely He took our infirmities and carried our sorrows, yet we considered Him stricken by God,

smitten by Him, and afflicted. But He was pierced for our transgressions, He was crushed for our iniquities; and the punishment that brought us peace was upon Him, and by His wounds we are healed." – Isaiah 53:4-5

We remember hearing the answers to all of our questions: Where we came from, why we are here, where are we going. Also, the promises of God were proclaimed: the forgiveness of sin, peace with God, and the assurance of everlasting life. It almost sounded too good to be true, when in life and religion everything of this nature has to be earned. The message brought forth was found in Ephesians 2:8-9: "For it is by grace that you have been saved, through faith – and this not from yourselves, it is the gift of God – not by works, so that no one can boast." He also shared about the resurrection which proves that Jesus is the Messiah.

"Jesus said, I am the resurrection and the life. He who believes in me will live, even though he dies; and whoever lives and believes in me will never die." – John 11:25

The service concluded with a Hymn, "Just As I Am." The pastor shared from John 3:3, "Unless a man is born again, he cannot see the kingdom of God."

While the congregation sang, he invited people to come to the altar to receive Jesus into their lives. The sanctuary and balcony were filled to capacity, with an overflow of people in the foyer. All four verses of the hymn were completed and not one person went forward. The pastor, being led by the Spirit made the invitation one more time, and the first verse was sung again. He said if you want to be born again, receive forgiveness of sin, peace in your heart and eternal life, now is the time to come. Without any discussion between us, I turned to Cher and asked if she would like to go forward. She said yes, and without further delay, we immediately stood up and walked down the red carpet to receive the Lord.

We prayed the sinner's prayer, confessing that Jesus is the Messiah, repenting of our sins, believing that he died and rose again from the grave. My Jewish upbringing was not destroyed but fulfilled. Jesus said he did not come to destroy the Law but to fulfill it. One of the misunderstandings among the Jewish people is, if you believe in Jesus that you are no longer a Jew. However, the Messiah was promised to the Jewish people. He Himself had to be Jewish, of the tribe of Judah, and the house of David, according to prophecy. All of the first followers of Jesus called "Christians" were Jewish. It's interesting to note that these Jewish followers of Jesus did not want to share the message of eternal life in the Jewish Messiah with Gentiles. Jesus fulfilled all of the prophecies concerning the Messiah in the Old Testament.

As a Jewish boy, there was no conflict when I realized that all the promises concerning the Messiah were made by Jewish people to the Jewish people.

Cher's upbringing was now understood. She believed in Jesus but never had personally invited Him into her life until this time. We experienced the true Shalom of the Lord. To our surprise, Cher's family in attendance that day had also come forward from a different location of the church. What a beautiful moment, without planning it, we all received the Lord together.

Four years later we would walk down that same aisle and become man and wife!

CHAPTER 3

WHAT DID I BELIEVE?

Fulfilling Our Religious Obligation ...

MIKE'S STORY

The blast of the shofar sounded and from behind the altar, unseen by the congregation, the choir sang in a Hebrew tongue. The rabbi stood at the pulpit and began to share his message. I wondered what all this meant. I was raised in the East Oak Lane neighborhood of Philadelphia, an only son with an older sister, Amy, and a younger sister, Jennifer, in a reformed Jewish home. Throughout my early childhood years I attended Sunday School at Temple Judea on Broad Street. In addition, I later went to Hebrew school during the week. All of this was in preparation for my Bar Mitzvah (which means "son of God's commandment"). I remember being so nervous about speaking in front of people, that I began these lessons a year early.

We observed the High Holy days by attending services, and celebrating the feasts at home including Passover, and Yom Kippur. My parents always took such pride in their family, and these times together. Their home was always fragranced with the beautiful fresh flowers adorning the elegance of china and silverware aligning the long dining room table. Much love and work went into these occasions.

On Passover we went to the bread box removing the loaves, and hiding them in the freezer, in an attempt to cleanse the house from leaven, (a symbol of sin). We would have our annual family get together to have the Seder, to remember the suffering and miraculous deliverance of the Jewish people. I now have the privilege of leading the service at my parent's home until this day. As a child, the high point of the holiday was searching for the afikoman, which would be rewarded with money to the child who found it. This brought much excitement to the young ones as they scattered throughout the home, looking all around to hopefully be the one to find it, and then receive their reward.

It's interesting to note that on every Passover table there are three whole pieces of matzah. The middle one is then removed, broken in half, wrapped in a cloth, and hidden to later be redeemed. This tradition reveals the mystery of the Trinity, God revealing Himself as Father, Son, and Holy Spirit. Elohim, as in Genesis 1:26, is where the plurality of God in personality is shown. One God expressed Himself in three ways. I liken it to a triangle, with three distinct and equal angles, all-encompassing one. One thing I knew for sure, as I was a young boy, that there is one God, and we do not bow down to idols. I never forgot that!

The afikoman, the Messiah, second person of the Trinity is represented by the middle matzah. He was broken as Isaiah 53 describes, He was sacrificed, buried and then resurrected from the dead. Isaiah 53:5 reads: "He was pierced for our transgressions, he was crushed for our iniquities, the punishment that brought us peace was upon him, and by his wounds we are healed."

> *"God made him who had no sin to be sin for us, so that in him we might become the righteousness of God." – 2 Corinthians 5:21*

> *"Get rid of the old yeast that you may be a new batch without yeast – as you really are. For Messiah Jesus, our Passover lamb, has been sacrificed." – 1 Corinthians 5:7*

Now my search for the afikoman (satisfying portion) has ended because I have found that Yeshua (Hebrew for Jesus) is the Messiah promised to the Jews, the true Passover Lamb.

On Yom Kippur, the Day of Atonement, we would fast and attend services as a sign of repentance. The family would gather at sun-down to break the fast with a special meal, which always included bagels and fish, and mom's specialties. Biblically, this was the one day the Jewish High Priest would enter the Holy of Holies with a blood sacrifice to atone for the sins of the nation. Since 70 A.D. with the destruction of the Temple, the blood sacrifices have ceased.

This is the question: How can our sin that separates us from God be covered without the animal sacrifice and offering of blood?

The answer is they can't be.

> *"For the life of a creature is in the blood, and I have given it to you to make atonement for yourselves on the altar; it is the blood that makes atonement for one's life." – Leviticus 17:11*

The Messiah came not just to cover our sins, but as prophesied, to remove them completely by His sacrifice.

> *"Such a high priest meets our need – one who is holy, blameless, pure, set apart from sinners, exalted above the heavens. Unlike the other high priests, he does not need to offer sacrifices day after day, first for his own sins, and then for the sins of the people. He sacrificed for their sins once for all when he offered himself."*
> *– Hebrews 7:26-27*

Scripture reveals that on our own we could never enter the presence of a Holy, righteous God, no matter how much good we have done. One imperfection keeps us out of His presence, and in a lifetime they add up very quickly. The good news is that although we deserve judgment, God has extended His mercy to us, to those who call upon His name. That is the true Shalom of God.

During one service at my synagogue I recall the Rabbi saying, "Some Jewish people believe the scriptures are directly inspired from God, and there are others that believe the words of the Bible are legends or myths." In my mind, I had hoped that he would have a more concrete answer. Here was a man that would surely know, yet his reply was that you can choose what you want to believe.

This left me with no answer and a dreaded feeling of uncertainty in the pit of my stomach. I had expected the Rabbi, who was the spiritual leader of the congregation, to reveal God's truth to me. With my many years of Jewish education, I was not shown the promises of God concerning the Messiah, heaven, and our future deliverance from death and judgment. On the Jewish holidays we would have a day off of school and attend services. I remember sitting in the back with my friends, and looking at our watch waiting for it to be over. We were fulfilling our religious obligation by being there, but we were not getting anything out of it. The service was ritualistic, and did not keep my attention.

I will never forget the first time I read the New Testament, that my reaction was the same as the Jewish people of the first century. When they heard Jesus speak, they said, "Here is a man that spoke with authority." Jesus said "Today, these scriptures are fulfilled in your hearing." As I talked among the other members of my Hebrew class, we discussed the incident of a girl who was called to the Rabbi's office because she said she did not believe in God. With all the chatter, even at this early age, I realized I had to come to grips with the answer to the question, "What did I believe?"

The truth is, I didn't know. As we continued to go to synagogue, I memorized the prayers and participated in responsive reading, fulfilling what was expected of me.

At the age of 13, the day of my Bar Mitzvah arrived. On that morning, before the service began, I was invited to the rabbi's office for the first time. He shared words of encouragement to me, because I was very nervous. When it was time for me to speak, I approached the pulpit, and quoted the special prayer before reading the scriptures both in Hebrew and in English. A ceremony is performed with the highest respect and reverence for God's Word, the Torah, which is the first five books of the Bible. As the organ music is heard and the choir sings, the Rabbi removes the Torah from the Ark where it is kept behind the pulpit. At this time the special engraved coverings and the jeweled encrusted ornaments are removed. The scrolls are then opened and the Rabbi hands me the silver pointer and I begin to read my scripture portion found in Numbers chapter 11:25-29. After reading in Hebrew, I translated into English and said the prayer after reading the scriptures.

My parents, family and the Rabbi were all pleased. I quoted everything that I was told to remember, but still did not know the meaning of what I was saying. After the service everyone was invited to a country club in Jenkintown for the celebration. A band was hired to play music throughout the day, and food and drink were plentiful.

It seemed that there was more emphasis on a party afterwards, and the excitement of going home to add up all of the gifts that I had received. Don't get me wrong, this certainly was part of the celebration, but my deepest thoughts and desires were still at unrest.

Not by coincidence, the scripture portion that I had read was from Numbers, which carried the message that all of God's people are to be prophets, His spokesman. Little did I know then, not comprehending it at the time, I would fulfill my Bar Mitzvah text by my life's calling.

During this celebration, our housekeeper Virgie, (who we considered part of our family), asked me if I believed in the Old Testament or the New Testament. With all of my Jewish education, I did not have an answer for her, and did not know the difference between the Old Covenant and the promise of a better one. Jeremiah 31:31: "The time is coming," declares the Lord, "when I will make a new covenant with the house of Israel and with the house of Judah."

I was fulfilling what Isaiah said ... I had the words memorized and coming out of my mouth, but they were far from my heart. Isaiah 29:13 reads: The Lord says: "These people come near to me with their mouth and honor me with their lips, but their hearts are far from me. Their worship of me is made up only of rules taught by men."

After I had completed my Bar Mitzvah, many of my classmates stopped attending synagogue, which was an option for me as well. My mom informed me that there was another alternative called Confirmation. It included three years of classes, some with the Rabbi, culminating with a celebration service where I would be confirmed a Jew. With all of my unanswered spiritual questions, this sounded interesting, so I immediately enrolled.

During the decade of the 70's there were many cults and philosophies enticing people through the medium of music, movies, and pop culture. I began playing the guitar, and listening to rock bands of the day. I was simply mesmerized by the sound of the guitar. I was unaware of the message in the music that was encouraging transcendental meditation and Eastern Mysticism. At this time Hare Krishna's were selling flowers, and the Moonies were soliciting donations. The artists were singing about peace and love, but had no answers.

I still felt unfulfilled and without direction.

As a Philly boy, I enjoyed my cheesesteaks from Pizza Palace, hoagies from Lee's, Peanut Butter Tasty Kakes, and soft pretzels. Watching and playing sports were other interests of mine. My hometown teams were the Flyers (Hockey), Eagles (Football), Phillies (Baseball) and the 76'ers (Basketball). So I was a well-rounded teen, and even thought maybe I would be a sports figure, or a rock star. I did not have a specific direction, but as I matured I knew I wanted to help people in some way. I was told of the importance of a good education, with the purpose of securing a job, and earning enough money to be self-sufficient.

I knew there had to be a deeper purpose than to just work to make money, but did not know what it was. Looking back, I know it was the Lord speaking to me. As a young boy listening to the Rabbi sharing about his experience to study to be a Rabbi, I felt a stirring in my spirit. Now I know it was the voice of the Lord calling me at an early age.

During the three years of confirmation classes we learned about Kabbalah, and studied comparative religion as our curriculum. Since the Bible was not the foundation for teaching, there were many different ideas and opinions that were offered. One of our teachers invited us to a Hare Krishna feast, but I did not attend.

Each week we attended various churches, and discussed the contrasts in belief. To me it seemed the main difference was that as Jews we called our creator God, and Christians called him Jesus (God becoming a man – not a separate deity.)

> *"For to us a child is born, to us a son is given, and the government shall be upon his shoulders,*

and he will be called Wonderful, Counselor, Mighty God, Everlasting Father, and the Prince of Peace." – Isaiah 9:6

Believe it or not, because of my interest in music, I brought the Rock Opera Jesus Christ Superstar into my confirmation class, and we listened to portions of it. We even had a presentation at our synagogue by a group who called themselves Hebrew Christians, who shared that Jesus was the Messiah promised to the Jews according to the Torah and Tanach. These were Jewish men and women who had placed their faith in Yeshua (Jesus) as their Messiah. There are many different terms for Jewish people who believe in Jesus: Messianic Jews, completed Jews, and Hebrew Christians. They gave each of us a prophecy edition of the New Testament, which I put in my secret compartment of my desk drawer, but never read. I completed the three years of study, being confirmed a Jew.

But I still did not know the answers to the questions. Why am I here? Where am I going?

For generations, all of my relatives came from a Jewish background. On my dad's side the family emigrated from Lithuania. I discovered that before coming to America, our last name was Love. The name of the family that sponsored them to come to the United States was Goldbloom, so they took on that name. In all actuality I am "Pastor Love"!

While in Europe my great-grandparents were orthodox Jews; my grand-mother raised my dad and uncle conservative. My parents attended a reform synagogue, so there was a trend, departing from biblical Judaism to traditional. On mom's side of the family members came from Russia and Germany. My grand-father was the president of a construction company in Philadelphia, where he and my grand-mother lived. The architectural design of their home was a Spanish Mission style, with white stucco walls and red tiled roof. The porch stretched across the whole front of the house with huge white columns accented by Greek scripted scrolls on top of them.

With Jewish ancestry on both sides of the family, something supernatural had to occur for me to one day believe Jesus is the Messiah.

CHAPTER 4
VIRGIE

Virgie Lived To See The Fruit Of Her Labor In My Life ...

While my grand-father lived on 11th Street, he had a housekeeper named Virgie. She lived with my grand-parents from Monday through Friday, and went home to her humble home in North Philly on week-ends. After I was born, my grand-father moved to New Jersey, and my parents moved into his home on 11th Street. Virgie became a part of our family. I feel more comfortable referring to her in that way, rather than as an employee, because of her special love for me. As far back as I can remember Virgie was concerned for my well-being. When my mom was at work, Virgie would always make sure I was dressed properly, and would always tell me to make sure "my sides were tucked in" and had "stockings on my feet."

She loved me enough to discipline me, and one time as a little boy held me upside down with one hand by my ankle, and with a wet wash rag in her other hand she said, "She was gonna whoop my handpot." She never hit me, but I received the message, and the fear of God!

I can't share my story, or how I came to faith in Jesus without talking about her. I did not understand it back then, but Virgie considered herself an apostolic prophetess. She was raised in Virginia on a cotton plantation, and only went to school until the fourth grade. She told me she learned to read by reading the Bible. As a young person, she was in an accident resulting in some type of serious neck injury (with some paralysis).

She made a deal with God, that if He would heal her, she would serve Him for the rest of her life; and she did. Many people will point to hypocrites in the church, as an excuse for why they do not want to walk with the Lord. But because of Virgie's Godly example and character, when I was old enough to understand, I had no excuse. As far as the world is concerned, she had no earthly treasures, and yet was always filled with joy. In the evenings, after preparing our meals and then cleaning up, I remember the sound of the dish washer and the lights dimmed. Virgie would sit at the end of the table to eat her meal by herself. Before she began eating, she would fold her hands and bow her head to bless the food in silent prayer.

One time as a pre-schooler, while Virgie was ironing clothes in the basement I could hear her talking out loud. Whenever she heard me approaching, she would always say, "I'm gonna call the police. I don't know where Mahcal (Michael) is." Then she would act surprised when she saw me. At other times, while she was doing her work, I could hear her voice. She would express to me that she was not crazy, I am not talking to myself, I'm talking to God. This left a powerful impact on me, because we as Jews memorized and recited prayers on special occasions. We talked about God, but Virgie talked to Him.

Since we were Jewish and Virgie was a Christian, she was instructed by my parents not to talk about Jesus, and could only read her Bible in her bedroom on the third floor.

When the Spirit would move her, she obeyed the Lord. She would talk to me in parables, which I did not understand as a child, but I totally understand now. She spoke about the authority of God, the Father, that He gave to His Son Jesus. She told me that because my father was at work, and away from the house, I (as the only son), was in charge. She proceeded to say that if I wanted her to leave for any reason, I had the authority to do so.

This was confusing to me at that time because I thought, "Why would I want to fire her, especially with how well she treated me?" In her Godly wisdom she was teaching me about the authority that Jesus now has on the earth. On another occasion, she was sending a prayer request to Oral Roberts, and pretended to need my help to address the letter.

She was teaching me, when you receive from a ministry, "You should give an offering;" and she would place one dollar with her prayer request and put it in the envelope.

As a boy, I would remember having nightmares and walking in my sleep. One night I remember waking up and Virgie was standing over me, praying in the Spirit. She later shared this story at a church I attended years ago. She laughed as she gave this testimony of praying for me, and I yelled out "Don't you do that no more...don't you do that no more!" As a little boy, I did not understand about praying in tongues and it frightened me. Imagine waking up from a bad dream with a heavy set black woman leaning over your bed, with her hands on your forehead, speaking in a language that you did not understand!

Now I cherish the thought of her prayers in my time of need. She had been planting seeds of the Gospel that have now sprung up; not only into faith, but ministry as well. Virgie lived to see the fruit of her labor, in my life.

When I was a teenager, and came home from school for lunch with my friends, Virgie would say, "The mod squad is here! One white, one black, and one blonde", then she would prepare our favorite sandwiches. (Cheese steaks) She was always attentive to our wants and needs. At night she would also come into my room and watch television with me, especially when I was watching the Flyers (ice hockey). Since there were always fist fights she called it "Lightly battles," not ice hockey and would chuckle.

We believe in doctors, and know that healing is from God, but when Virgie got sick she would pray and fast. I remember mom calling up from the second floor into the darkness of her room, pleading for her to go to the doctors. Virgie would reply with, "I am praying and fasting." She taught me by example how to walk by faith, and to call upon the Lord in my time of need.

> *"A righteous man may have many troubles, but the Lord delivers him from them all."*
>
> *– Psalm 34:19*

Virgie opened up her home for worship services on Saturday and Sundays. After I was called into the ministry, this was the first place I preached on 27th Street, one block south of Lehigh. On the side of her corner row house it said, "Jesus Never Fails", and we have found that out to be true.

Since I saw Virgie live the Christian life day to day, she wanted me to be the one to preach her funeral, and that it would be a day of celebration not sadness. Twenty-seven years ago, when Virgie was 77, what an honor it was to carry out her wishes. When I saw her earthly tabernacle lying there in the casket, there was no question that Virgie was with the Lord. Even though Virgie is not physically here on the earth, her testimony is still alive because of the impact she had on my life.

"By faith Abel offered God a better sacrifice than Cain did. By faith he was commended as a righteous man, when God spoke well of his offerings. And by faith he still speaks, even though he is dead." – Hebrews 11:4

CHAPTER 5

On A Quest To Know Him More...

CHER'S STORY

I was born in Philadelphia, but spent most of my childhood in the suburbs with my mom and three brothers, Joe, Rick, and Marshall. My parents did not remain married, but they remain friends. My dad is Catholic and my mom is from a Protestant background.

I learned about Jesus at an early age, and always was on a quest to know Him more. I just did not know how to go about doing this. There was always a peace that would come over me when I would think of Him. I remember having home-made communion as a little girl, placing the elements on the living room window sill. As I would partake of the emblems, while looking outside, I marveled at His creation. There was always a sense of awe and feeling of warmth in my heart at those times.

I recall singing in the car with my mom and brothers, the hymn "Holy, Holy, Holy", as she was driving down the road. There was something powerful about those words! When my dad took me to church, it just reaffirmed the faith that I had, and my love for Jesus.

I also was developing an interest in the performing arts. Music seemed to be a healer and could take you away for a while. As a child I was accepted into a Children's Repertory Theater on Spruce Street in Philadelphia. Every Saturday and Sunday I would go to rehearse. Then we would perform our shows to the public. As I became a teen I had a vocal coach at the Shubert Theater, who was preparing me to work as a soloist in a future band for a career. I also was involved with other theater productions, winning awards such as the "Performing Arts Award" for our local Junior Miss pageant.

During the competition I was able to share my faith by answering the question: "What movie has influenced your life the most?" I thought I would ruin my chance for winning, but I was compelled to share regardless of the consequences. I made a promise to God that no matter what, I would give Him the glory. Up until that point the movie that had affected me the most was "The Thief in the Night", which spoke about the Lord's return. There I was in this large auditorium, with hundreds of people staring at me, talking about being prepared for the Lord's return. I remember walking away and saying to myself, "Okay, Lord, I did it."

After talking about Jesus in this way, I was very surprised when they called out my name to receive the performing arts award. I had planned to continue my education and eventually have some type of singing/acting career. There was much excitement, and yet something was missing. I loved my music, and yet the search was on.

The 70's were not easy times. There were many decisions that had to be made. I felt at times I was in the world, but not of it. What does all of this mean? What is my purpose? I know there has to be more than just living, and then dying.

I had some knowledge of my Lord, and yet did not know how personal this relationship could be, and would eventually be. When I finally realized that I needed to know Him as Lord and Savior, and to personally receive Him into my life, the questions started being answered. But now what do I do with this music, my singing career? Again, decisions had to be made, and the pull to get closer to God was growing.

As you hear our story, and think back upon your life, look for the people that God has placed there, to draw you to Himself. It is His kindness that leads us to repentance.

CHAPTER 6
BEGINNING OF OUR WALK WITH THE LORD

My Parent's Reaction Would Be Explosive...

After receiving our Messiah Jesus, we had a deep desire to grow spiritually and a hunger for His Word. We continued to go to church each Sunday. I would leave my home early Sunday morning from East Oak Lane, Philadelphia, and then pick up Cher who lived in the suburbs. We attended Sunday School with Cher's mom. Even though we were teenagers, we were in the Sporty Forties class. The teacher was dynamic and many of the friends we met then are still a part of our family even today. After Sunday School, we would go to the worship service. It was all so new to us, and we wanted as much as we could receive in this new relationship with the Lord.

Later that year we learned that there would be a Water Baptism Service. Although Mikvah (water baptism) is a Jewish act of repentance, it was new to me. I felt like a spy leaving my home, in the middle of winter, smuggling a towel and bathing suit without my parent's knowledge. I was not ready to reveal my new found faith in Messiah. I knew where my parent's stood as far as Jesus is concerned, and their reaction would be explosive. I understood where they were coming from since all they knew is what they were taught. Each candidate was asked to share a scripture, and to give a brief testimony.

I remember saying, "I was a completed Jew," and shared Revelation 3:20: "Here I am! I stand at the door and knock. If anyone hears my voice and opens the door, I will go in and eat with him, and he with me." After being immersed in water, and taking my first breath, I felt as though I could fly. I know our salvation is not dependent on feeling because we are saved by faith alone. However, at that moment I felt as light as a feather. There was a sense of freedom to publicly declare that Jesus was my Messiah.

> *"Whoever acknowledges me before men, I will also acknowledge him before my father in heaven." – Matthew 10:32*

Wanting to surprise me and get something special, Cher purchased a gold Jewish Star and had the jeweler place a cross in the center. This became a symbol of the fulfillment of my Jewish faith. In the mid-seventies men wore silk shirts, opened at the chest so the pendant would jump out at you. At this point in my walk with the Lord I would button my shirt up before I arrived home, so it would not be visible to my family.

While we were attending this church, we heard about a ministry in Ambler, Pennsylvania called the Christian Cinema. Every Friday and Saturday evening they showed movies free of charge, with a Gospel message. As teenagers, we started attending every week-end. This was a tremendous support to our spiritual growth, and we met many people from various backgrounds and denominations who loved the Lord. This also excited Cher to see the movie medium being used in a positive way, and encouraged her to use her gifts to reach out to others as well as glorify the Lord.

One of these nights, while we were at the Cinema, the invitation was given for people to volunteer to clean the theater each week. Hundreds of people attended, and the building needed to be prepared for the arrival of the crowds for the next showing. There was a stirring within us to be used of the Lord. Without much Biblical knowledge, this was something we knew we could do, and we began going each week with anticipation to help. I remember the first time we went, after the work was finished, we sat down in a circle to share dessert. But first… one by one, they offered up a prayer. I had never prayed out loud in public before. As my turn was near, I was so nervous my eyelids were fluttering. My mouth moved, and words came out, but I could not tell you what that prayer was. This was the beginning of our public ministry.

After doing this for many months, we were asked to help out behind the counter selling popcorn and candy. We loved being able to welcome people and to be involved in the Lord's work. We volunteered throughout our teenage and early adult years. Eventually we were able to become ushers, and altar workers. After the salvation invitation was given, we shared the scriptures assuring them of their decision to follow the Lord.

Over the years we had brought many family members and friends to come watch the movies, and almost all of them received Jesus. This sparked even a greater desire to grow in ministry, and for our lives to be used for Him. We did not know the lingo, "the calling of the Lord", or what "full-time" ministry meant. We began to learn that every believer is called to serve and use their gifts. Eventually, we would understand, some are called to a full-time position in the ministry.

Since I was living at home, and my parents did not know about my faith, I decided to finish college with a business degree. My plan was that after graduation, I could then secure a job, and Cher and I would get married, and serve the Lord as He led us. I graduated from Philadelphia Textiles and Sciences, which is now Philadelphia University. I majored in accounting and minored in psychology, which turns out to be a big advantage in the ministry.

In Cher's senior year of high school, my family was invited to the graduation ceremony.

For her last year she attended Phil-Mont Christian Academy, at the time located in Dresher, Pennsylvania. The ceremony was held at the Westminster Seminary.

Cher had been asked to sing for this event. She chose the song, "Jesus is the Answer," by Andre Crouch.

The lyrics proclaim that Jesus is the answer for the world today…above Him there's no other…Jesus is the way. Cher wanted to use this as an opportunity to express her faith, and to use her gift of singing. This was just the beginning of open doors for service.

Later that night, when everyone was preparing for bed, my mom said to me, "I did not know Cher was that religious." and then asked, "You're not a Christian … are you?" I was completely caught off guard, and immediately blurted out … NO! I was not ready for the persecution, and just like Peter, I heard "the rooster crow."

During this time, we had heard, but not experienced what it meant to be filled with the Spirit. We read about it in the Bible, heard testimonies of what God was doing, attended Spirit-filled prayer meetings and revival services. Cher's mom was the first to share her experience with us. This encouraged us to seek the Baptism of the Holy Spirit for ourselves. Knowing it was real, we wanted all that God had to give. When we first accepted the Lord we received the indwelling presence of the Holy Spirit.

> *"Because you are sons, God sent the Spirit of His Son into our hearts, the Spirit who calls out Abba Father." – Galatians 4:6*

In the first chapter of the book of Acts, Jesus told His disciples not to leave Jerusalem, but to wait for the gift the Father promised. Acts 1:5 says, "For John baptized with water, but in a few days you will be baptized with the Holy Spirit." The word baptize means "to immerse." That's why during water baptism they were immersed in the Jordan River. Jesus promised to immerse us with the Holy Spirit, and we knew we had not received that experience yet, but hungered for it.

In seeking this gift, I was encouraged to spend more time alone with the Lord. Instead of petitioning the Lord for things, I began to praise Him and thank Him for who He is. With my third floor bedroom door closed, I would kneel before the Lord with my Bible opened on the bed. This was the miniature prophecy edition of the New Testament that was hidden away in my secret compartment of my desk drawer, given to me by the Hebrew Christians that came to my synagogue years before.

Whenever I began to worship like this, I began to literally feel the presence of the Lord. My face would become numb with a tingling sensation, and the peace of God flooded my soul. There was a steady increase of the recognizable presence of the Lord in my life. Since I was not able to outwardly confess my faith to those in my household, these times alone with the Lord were very special. During a time of worship at home and encouragement from a 700 Club telephone counselor, I began to pray in the Spirit, "speaking in tongues." With this new prayer and praise language I experienced a greater awareness of God's presence and I was empowered to confess my faith to my family.

> *"But you will receive power when the Holy Spirit comes on you; and you will be my witnesses in Jerusalem, and in all Judea and Samaria, and to the ends of the earth." – Acts 1:8*

One day at the kitchen table, I had what seemed to be an "out of body" experience. I was sitting at one end of the rectangular table, and my mom and dad were at the other end. In one breath, I told them that I was a born-again Christian, and engaged to Cher. To say the least, the reaction was like a mushroom cloud that rose from the table. Voices got loud; and calls for my "de-programming" and need to see a psychologist were made.

There had to be something wrong for me to need something that they could not give me. At one time I would have stood to my feet and raised my voice along with them, in my defense, but I now experienced a peace that only God could give and remained in control. I understand, once being in unbelief, why they reacted the way they did. I was the only son in this Jewish family, and the only one in my lineage who believed this.

Now that my eyes were opened, I received the revelation that Jesus is the Messiah, foretold about by the Jewish prophets. The scriptures declare that Jesus came to his own people the Jews, but they did not receive Him. The same is true in my life.

Shortly after we received the Lord our Pastor stepped down from his position after some accusations. My mom discovered it on the front page of the Philadelphia Inquirer, hoping this would cause me to stop going to church. However, this did not surprise us, or shake us in our newly-found faith. We were not following a man, and our trust was in God alone.

Often while I was still living at home, my mom would try to tell me things such as Christians hate the Jews and Jesus can't be the answer to all of life's problems. My response was simple, because I had received nothing but love from Gentile believers in Jesus, and discovered that Jesus is the answer to all life's problems. My parents tried to stop my spiritual growth on every side. When I would order books from ministry programs through the mail, I would find them in the bottom of the trash can.

When I told them I was thinking of going to Bible school, my dad and his employer tried to recruit me into the life insurance business, saying this was God's work to help people. As a teenager, I remember driving in the car with my younger sister Jennifer, and sharing about my faith in Messiah Jesus. She immediately told me that I had to stop talking about Jesus, because mom and dad had forbidden such discussions.

When we would be at family gatherings, friends as well as relatives would gladly engage in spiritual conversations with us. But whenever my mom discovered this, she would interrupt and tell us to change the conversation. Whenever someone was sick or in the hospital, this kind of information was withheld from us, because my parents knew we would immediately go to visit them and offer prayer.

One time, after the funeral of a close Jewish friend I grew up with, who committed suicide, I was then told he was having problems. Obviously, too late to go share the good news of the Gospel with him. Our response to this persecution that sprang solely from my faith in Jesus was to continue to love them and use wisdom in when to verbally share our faith and when to show it by action.

For decades, the Lord directed us to show our faith by continuing to attend all of the Jewish holidays, and to let our actions speak louder than words. The Holy Spirit guided us through these years, as we gave them books, invited them to special services, and shared what God was doing in our lives. My parents, years later, attended Shalom for our celebration service, and began to see the good in what we were doing by bringing people together, both Jew and Gentile. They even respected my position addressing letters to me as "Reverend" Mike Goldbloom.

They also started to introduce me as their son,

Pastor Mike Goldbloom, and approved me to perform weddings and funerals for family members. God was working on their hearts, too!

One night while Cher was in deep prayer, consecrating her life to the Lord in her bedroom, as she was speaking the words out in English, the Spirit began to pray through her in "tongues." She said it was as though her whole being was enveloped in the warmth of God's Holy love. There was a sense of awe that surrounded her and she didn't want it to end.

> *"The Spirit helps us in our weakness. We do not know what we ought to pray, but the Spirit Himself intercedes for us, with groans that words cannot express." "and He who searches our hearts, knows the mind of the Spirit, because the Spirit intercedes for the saints in accordance with God's will." – Romans 8:26-27*

We learned we had to be tactful, because many Christians we knew did not understand about this experience. At 18 years of age, we were sharing this with those who were hungry for more of God and His power. Some rejected it flat out, because of their own upbringing and teaching. We knew it was Biblical and could not deny the effect that it had on our lives.

Cher and I began singing together for weddings, and started traveling to different churches, sharing our testimony and music. We called it "Music With A Message." Opportunities opened up for us to go to

Catholic, Baptist, Assembly of God, Methodist, Messianic congregations, to name a few. We ministered at "Love Banquets," Passover Seders, coffeehouses, youth groups, women's conferences, and main services. We were sensing that this calling for full-time ministry could very well be something that the Lord would have for us some day.

One of the confirmations for this was when a bar owner (that got saved) gave us the sound system from the club for our ministry. God was just beginning to show His favor to us as we honored Him. He gave us two home-made speakers and a PA system. At that time we had a used sky blue Chevy Chevette for transportation. The speakers were so big, and the car so small that with the back seat folded down we could only fit one speaker at a time. Sometimes we borrowed a neighbor's van until we finally purchased a portable sound system that we still use for concerts today.

> *"Well done, my good servant!" his master replied. "Because you have been trustworthy in a very small matter, take charge of ten cities."*
>
> *– Luke 19:17*

Zechariah 4:10 reads: "Who despises the day of small things?"

Don't despise small beginnings. He wants to use you just the way you are, right where you are. Step out of the boat of comfort and the opportunities for service will present themselves.

"I know your deeds. See I have placed before you an open door that no one can shut."

– Revelation 3:8

CHAPTER 7
OUR WEDDING

Fulfilling God's Plan For This Hour...

From the time we accepted the Lord, along with this new found joy we had received, also came a deep desire for our families to know Him. We could not keep such a great salvation to ourselves! Isaiah 55:11 promises that every time the seed of the Word of God is planted, it never returns empty, but will bring forth a harvest of spiritual fruit.

We knew our wedding day would be an opportunity for all of our loved ones to hear the Good News message. We wanted it to be proclaimed in a simple, understandable way.

During this time, our church was in the midst of a pastoral change. When we went to meet with the new pastor, we shared our intent and purpose for our wedding that we desired.

Thinking everything was taken care of, when final plans were discussed with my family, a problem ensued. Due to their Jewish background, they emphatically declared they would not attend a wedding or invite family and friends, if it was going to be a "Billy Graham Crusade." They did not even want the name of Jesus to be mentioned.

Now we were at an impasse. For years we desired our wedding to be a great witness and testimony of our faith, and now at the last minute we find out my family may not be attending. As a result, we set up another meeting with the new pastor, which my dad wanted to attend. At this meeting we would discuss the specific content of the wedding ceremony. The pastor from our previous get together knew our desire, but when my dad expressed his concerns, about the name of Jesus, he agreed with him. On the outside Cher and I remained calm, but on the inside we felt our mouth's drop to the floor, as if to say, "What did he just say?" and that gnawing pit in our stomach thinking all of our hopes and great expectations of this glorious day seemed to vanish; when both families would finally be together to hear of so great a salvation. We left the meeting just shaking our heads.

Even when we don't understand what God is doing, He always has all things under control. There may be times in your life when you question why things have turned out the way that they have. Remember he is not finished working on your behalf.

> *"For my thoughts are not your thoughts, neither are your ways, my ways declares the Lord. As the heavens are higher than the earth, so are my ways higher than your ways, and my thoughts than your thoughts." – Isaiah 55:8-9*

Now that dad was satisfied with the outcome of the meeting, the approval was given for the invitations to be sent out to their family and friends. We were glad that they were going to attend our wedding ceremony, but disappointed in how dreams seemed to be shattered.

We had waited years for this day, and wondered now, where will God get the glory.

The countdown had begun, and it was just weeks before the wedding day. Cher received a call from the church secretary. She was very pleasant and reassuring, with the news she was about to share. She apologized, but revealed to us that the Pastor who was to perform our ceremony became ill, and was going on sabbatical. The secretary, who was a member of another church, went on to say that her pastor would be perfect, and is willing to fill in to officiate our wedding. Cher knew immediately that God was moving, and this was no coincidence!! We set up an appointment and met with him, sharing the preceding events.

In meeting with him, there was an instantaneous witness in our spirits that he was the one to fulfill God's plan for this hour. He had a very gentle and kind persona, and understood our heart's desire. We didn't know exactly what he was going to say during the ceremony, but we were confident that this day now would be what we had prayed for. We left his office that day praising the Lord.

The day had arrived. Saturday, September 9, 1978, a beautiful sunny day. When Cher thinks of the morning hours, she remembers the brightness of the sky with a heavenly crystal blue color, causing us again to marvel at His creation. As I prepared for the day in prayer, I knew Cher would be getting ready with help from her mom, pictures would be taken, and her dad would be there to take her to the church.

Before the wedding service began, I met with the Pastor in the side room, next to the sanctuary. The first words out of his mouth were, "You wanted the Gospel; you're going to get the Gospel" (Good News). I remember such a peace filling up within. We see how God was the architectural designer and turned things completely around. Our families were both in attendance, and God was going to be praised.

From the first thoughts of planning our wedding, we wanted to include some of the Jewish traditions because they are meaningful.

I never lost my Jewishness by accepting Jesus as my Messiah.

As you entered the sanctuary doors, you couldn't help but notice the chuppah, (wedding canopy) at the center of the altar area. I am not sure if the church had ever had one before during a wedding ceremony. The chuppah represents the covering of God, and our submission to his authority. It also speaks of the Jewish home that is now being established. Underneath the chuppah was a prayer bench where Cher and I kneeled when the Pastor prayed his blessing upon us. My tuxedo was burgundy in color, as well as my best man and ushers (Popular color in the 70's). Cher's gown was white, with angel sleeves, and a veil covering her face. Her maid of honor was dressed in a pale pink gown, with a matching parasol that she held over her shoulder. The beautiful scent of gardenias filled the room. I also broke the glass under my heel after the ceremony, in celebration, another Jewish tradition. Just as the glass is shattered and cannot go back to its original form, symbolizing this new relationship of marriage which changes your life forever.

After the vows and exchange of rings, the Pastor brought forth a skillfully crafted message entitled "How is a Man Right with God."

He began with Abraham the father of the Jews, and said even though he was a "stinker" (sinner), he believed God, and it was credited to him as righteousness. Without an invitation to accept the Lord, the Pastor expressed God's plan of salvation through faith in Jesus as the Messiah for both Jew and Non-Jew..."the faith that Mike and Cher have embraced." In God's providence and plan, this was the same altar that four years earlier we committed our lives to the Lord, and now to each other. One of our songs was entitled "Each for the other, and both for the Lord."

The reception was held at the Highpoint Racquet Club in Chalfont, Pennsylvania, where Cher's dad was a member. We had a wonderful buffet dinner with about 300 in attendance. One of our friends played the accordion taking requests at each table. Virgie was there as well, and sang a hymn for us.

We later found out that my family was upset about the ceremony. They did not approve of us kneeling under the chuppah, or with the Pastor's message, among other things. Over 20 years after our wedding ceremony, the Pastor told me that my mom sent him a nasty letter because he called Abraham a "stinker." When Jesus, the Messiah came to His own town, his own family and brethren did not receive Him. How true it is that a prophet is without honor among his family.

Proverbs 3:5-6 has always been one of our life's scripture verses. It shows that when you put God first, He will work out circumstances, even when you do not understand what is taking place.

> *"Trust in the Lord with all your heart, and lean not on your own understanding; in all your ways acknowledge Him, and He will make your paths straight." – Proverbs 3:5-6*
>
> *"Commit your way to the Lord, trust in Him, and He will do this." – Psalm 37:5*

We Were At The End Of Our Rope – Then The Phone Rang!

Our first home, located in Glenside, Pennsylvania, was a step of faith. It was a two bedroom twin doll house, with a white picket fence, and wooden front porch. It was our prized possession. The kitchen was so narrow, if you opened the oven you had to stand sideways. It was connected to the dining room where our borrowed card table stood, (and only piece of furniture). The closets were so small you couldn't hang a hangar to close the door. Our main and only bathroom had a bathtub, surrounded by colors of pink and white pretend tile, without a shower, and when we moved in we found out our heater was condemned!! Our beautiful Paul Bunyan bedroom set that Cher's mom bought for us as a wedding present, had to be given back because it would not fit up the stairway. From this humble beginning, we felt blessed to have a home, and our priority was to serve the Lord.

My first job out of college was an auditing position at a bank. Cher continued medical clerical work and child care in our home. We also ministered on weekends, going from church to church, singing and sharing our testimony. One night we received a call from Cher's aunt, telling us about an Assembly of God church in Philadelphia, where they raised their hands and praised the Lord! The first Wednesday night we attended they had a guest Messianic singing group called "Psalms of David." There were about 15 people in attendance, but the presence of God was rich.

During our first year of marriage we continued attending this church, and had a weekly Bible study in our home. The more we got involved with ministry, the greater the hunger for the Lord grew. One night as we were in prayer for a physical healing for Cher, God's presence fell in an overwhelming way. The Holy Spirit came upon us, where we could hardly move because of the heaviness of His presence. This experience resulted in a physical healing for her, and a new awareness of God's call. Soon after this, while I was away on a business trip, I was called back to the office and told this was my last day. The company's president said, "Wining and dining business owners was not your bag" and I would be better suited for another career. At first I was shocked because this move was completely unexpected.

However, he did not know that the Lord was using him and confirming God's leading in our lives. Instead of coming home to share the bad news of a job loss, I came home excited and rejoicing knowing God was changing course. During the drive home a rainbow appeared reaffirming that God's promises would come to pass, even though we did not know the future. When

I arrived home and shared this with Cher, we both were in agreement that this was the time to launch out to follow our call to the full-time ministry. I knew it was my responsibility to support my family financially, but there was a continued dissatisfaction for me in secular employment. I remember Pat Robertson saying that if you are fulfilled in working a secular job, you are not "called." Since we had been involved with part-time ministry in and outside of the church, there was a stirring on the inside every time we heard about those who serve the Lord in full-time ministry. I met with the Pastor and his counsel was to go to Bible School and prepare.

The closest Assembly of God Bible School was Valley Forge Christian College in Phoenixville. By faith, I made the hour journey, and enrolled in the fall semester for Pastoral Studies. Without the money for tuition, no job, not eligible for unemployment, we were "walking on the water." In the physical realm, this did not make sense. However we believed that when God leads, he also provides. God called Abraham to leave his family and go to a place not specified. He had to be obedient to partial instruction from the Lord, before receiving full revelation.

This is where we were. At that time we had no family in ministry and no one in our church going to Bible school. We were simply following the leading of God's Spirit for us. When Jesus called Peter to get out of the boat to "walk on water," and literally do the impossible, Jesus didn't explain the how's and the why's. But when Peter was obedient, and kept his eyes on Jesus, he accomplished the miraculous. It did not matter what the other disciples were or were not doing. So, I began taking classes in the morning, studying in the afternoon, and looking for a part-time job in the evenings. Nothing opened up. We had no mentor in ministry to explain to us how to make the transition from the business world to ministry. Our mortgage and car payments were due. Tuition had not been paid, and we had run out of money. With no savings, we came to the point where a decision had to be made. Continue Bible school and get a part-time job, or quit school and go back to full-time secular employment.

Cher's boss offered me an interview for a position the following Monday. That Friday morning, during our chapel service at VFCC, a missions offering was taken. I felt led to give the last $5 in my pocket as a seed offering. No one knew our situation and that week-end we prayed specifically for direction.

After we came home from church that Sunday, we realized time was getting short, and we were at the end of our rope ... then the phone rang. The pastor of our church said someone had anonymously designated a $500 gift to us personally. In 1979, that was a lot of money. It was a confirmation to continue Bible School, and that week a second shift job opened up as a proofreader. The Lord was showing His provision, and we have never forgotten that.

"And my God will meet all your needs according to His glorious riches in Christ Jesus."
–Philippians 4:19

This is for you too. As you continue to sow, remember that if you don't give up, you will reap the harvest in due time. If you feel that you are being led in a specific area and it does not go away, then test to see if it is God's will by launching out in faith. It's easy to remain in the safety and comfort of the boat, but you will never know the thrill of victory unless you take that step.

Since the age of 16, when we accepted the Lord and learned of His ways, we have honored Him with tithes and offerings, of all our increase. He continues to open the windows of heaven and pour out His blessings.

"Bring the whole tithe into the storehouse, that there may be food in my house. Test me in this, says the Lord Almighty, and see if I will not throw open the floodgates of heaven and pour out so much blessing that you will not have room enough for it." – Malachi 3:10

CHAPTER 9
FOLLOWING GOD'S CALL

"God Is Going To Use You..."

In our early twenties we were involved in many ministries of our church. We were holding Bible studies in our home, music ministry from church to church, juggling between Bible school classes, studying, and working second and third shift jobs ... (including factory work, and management at McDonalds).

During this time I was offered a full-time sales job at a cemetery as a memorial counselor. This was another step of faith and trust in God as we progressed from a salaried position to commission only. I never had done sales before, but with God's help for the next five years our income increased each year. My responsibilities included going into homes to present the sales pitch to buy cemetery plots. I described to the people different locations of the cemetery grounds, which included the Bible section, The Good Shepherd, Woman at the Well, etc.

In the midst of the presentation, I would always get the question that this sounds like a Christian cemetery, "Aren't you Jewish?" This opened up the opportunity to share my testimony, and how to prepare for the end of earthly life and how to be prepared spiritually.

This certainly was great training grounds for pastoral experience, attending funerals, ministering to those grieving, and giving hope of eternal life. The job also included "duty days" where you manned the reception desk from morning until evening. On one of these days, as I was reading the scriptures, the passage in Genesis concerning Joseph jumped out. God had allowed Joseph to go through trying circumstances, to bring out His greater purpose.

The nation of Israel at that time was in severe famine, and in desperate need of miraculous provision for their existence to continue. Joseph was mistreated by his family, sold into slavery, falsely accused, imprisoned, forgotten and yet God continued to bless and prosper him in the midst of all these tests. What the enemy meant for evil, and his destruction, God turned it around and not only brought good, but provided for the entire nation of Israel.

> *"You intended to harm me, but God intended it for good to accomplish what is now being done, the saving of many lives" – Genesis 50:20.*

To accomplish this Joseph was promoted to second-in-command as Prime Minister under Pharaoh in Egypt, and he was 30 years old. While reading this, the Holy Spirit confirmed to my heart that my first full-time ministry position would be as the Assistant Pastor of our church that we had been attending; and I would be 30. This also brought back to my memory, the first time I read the New Testament as a Jewish believer, that Jesus began his ministry when he was 30. After continuing to work at the cemetery, I was hired at the church in that position, three months after my 30th birthday. Hallelujah!

During the years of preparing and waiting on the Lord, we had received many words of prophecy confirming God's call and plan. One time during revival services at church, I was last in line at the altar call for physical healing. The guest evangelist, who had never met me, instead of praying for my healing, began to prophesy repeatedly: "Study My Word, and preach the Gospel." Other prophecies by different people confirmed what we knew God wanted to do. "God was going to use us" and bring people from different backgrounds together.

We had gone to our first Pentecostal tent meeting in Fort Washington, Pennsylvania. When the service concluded the evangelist pointed his finger directly at me, and said, "God is going to use you." Another time, in church, a guest evangelist pointed to Cheryl and me, and told us to come forward. After coming to the front he said, "God is going to use you to reach multitudes and perform the miraculous." Years later, we attended a service where the prophet pointed at us and began prophesying that the road was hard, but God was going to send the cavalry. He was going to send people to support and strengthen the ministry.

We never saw this woman before and she did not know we were in the ministry. She went on to say under the inspiration of the Spirit, that she saw properties, and people from many ethnic backgrounds coming. She continued prophesying specifics that all came to pass. We recognized this was the voice of the Lord, and brought great encouragement in the midst of trials.

In August of 1987, at thirty years old, I was hired as the Assistant Pastor. My responsibilities included being a hospital chaplain, food bank, youth, teaching, preaching, forming a worship band, and cell group meetings in our home. That year we moved closer to the church, where we still presently live.

In this position I was thrilled to be serving the Lord, and to be in a supportive role to the Senior Pastor. We saw the church grow, people coming to the Lord, and we were excited to be a part of helping to build up this congregation. We thought we could be there until the Lord's return, but He had a different plan. It ended up being a time of training for future ministry.

During one of our in home cell group meetings, one of the ladies had a prayer request for surgery to take place the next morning. As we laid our hands upon her, and prayed the prayer of faith, we all recognized that God was doing something supernatural. She had to sit down because the presence of God was so strong. She was not able to have children.

The next morning, before the surgery, she called

screaming with excitement and joy, that the scar tissue clearly seen on the x-ray, had passed naturally. When she went for her procedure to be done, the doctors were amazed because nothing was there. Shortly after this time she conceived and had her first son. Through the years we have seen God answer our prayers specifically in this area, where families with fertility problems, now have many children. To God be the glory!

During this process of infertility and struggle, this woman's husband, who grew up as an atheist in East Germany came to know the Lord. When they tried to have another child, the doctor's diagnosed her with a rare disease which made it impossible to carry full-term.

She had gone to fertility specialists, however all procedures had failed. Then she called us to pray again, and she not only conceived, but bore their second son. Their names are Jonathan and David.

These miracles gave us a glimpse of what the Lord would continue to do, as we followed the direction and empowering of the Holy Spirit. Romans 8:14 says, "because those who are led by the Spirit of God are sons of God."

Expanding Our Capacity To Love...

As we continued to be led by the Spirit, we knew it was time for us to have our own children. We looked forward to raising them in faith and dedicating them to the Lord even before they were born. When the home pregnancy test was taken, and it was positive, Cher called me at her aunt's home where I was doing some painting. This news was so wonderful to hear. I brought home a rose for this memorable occasion. During the pregnancy Cher was very conscientious of everything she ate and drank, knowing it would affect the life growing inside of her (No medications, no caffeine, etc.). Even then there was the motherly instinct of protecting her child from any harm. She did have some cravings such as Roy Rogers' coleslaw, Howard Johnson's milkshakes, and caramel sundaes from McDonalds.

I did have what they call "sympathy pains." When she experienced some morning sickness, I did too, and as she started to gain weight, I made sure she was not alone. During the early 80's the technology was not like it is today with the 4D video where you can view the baby in the womb, but you could discover the gender if you so chose. We decided to be surprised, and to wait until the baby was born. We were just thankful for God's gift to us.

Not knowing what gender the baby would be, we felt the baby would be our Rachel, ("ewe," title of endearment "lamb" – in the Bible she was the mother of Joseph, Israel's Savior). We even called the spare bedroom "Rachel's Room." The pregnancy went very well, no complications, and we had taken natural childbirth classes, and I was the coach. The Lamaze classes were held at Chestnut Hill Hospital. They taught us the proper breathing techniques to help through the hard labor. I wanted to be there to do everything that I could to comfort and supply aid during the delivery (Such as offering lollipops or crushed ice).

We were anticipating the real birth. On Memorial Day, May 25th 1981, the Lord gave me a dream, where I was prophesying, "and you shall be filled with rivers of living water." At that moment, Cher woke up and revealed to me that her water had broken. Literally a river of water went forth. Joyfully, we rode the wave and were awakened!

After jumping up we started counting minutes between contractions. Recognizing we were in the urgency zone, we called the doctor who said, "Leave now!" We also were glad we packed a bag ahead of time, and cleaned the house. The doctor's due date had been a month later, but Cher had a keen sense during her pregnancy that he was off about a month, which was confirmed during her last doctor's visit, three days before.

When we arrived at the hospital, Cher was experiencing severe pain. She could only imagine what it would be like when it was time to give birth. While we were in the labor room the nurse asked if I wanted to see the baby's head. I said, "Sure", but when I looked, I was not prepared to see so much blood. Immediately my tongue became thick, my stomach and hands went numb, and I nearly fainted. It so happens, she was already nine centimeters, and it was time to move to the delivery room. We were 20 feet from this big event that we had prepared for, and I was almost restricted from the delivery room, because they were concerned that I may faint. For me this was an act of faith, and I told them I would be okay. While Cher was straining with the final push, my eyes focused on her, and not the actual delivery.

From the water breaking at 2:00 am, till the delivery at 5:57 am; it was very quick! Cher delivered 100% natural. I was there coaching her with breathing exercises and holding her hand. But Cher refused all offers of crushed ice and lollipops! What a celebration on this very hot Memorial Day. Rachel's Oma, (grand-mom) was born on May 30th the traditional day, so this was a double blessing for sure.

When Rachel was born and they put her in Cher's

arms, Cher said, "There was such a feeling of awe, I want to protect my baby girl and this overwhelming love in my heart was so strong and filled with joy. She is such a beautiful gift."

"Rachel" … One of Cher's distinct memories aside from lots of dark hair, were her long eyelashes that brushed against her rosy complexion. During her photo op at the hospital, Rachel was wrapped in a pink blanket, and the hospital team made mention that she looked like a little papoose. This miracle of love will be a part of our heart forever. She opened up a new part of our hearts, and expanded our capacity to love.

Everything was going smoothly, and when the discharge day was here, the hospital team gave us news that Rachel couldn't come home. As a young couple this was a shock, and we felt like someone punched us in the stomach. She had jaundice (which to us as new parents, sounded a lot worse than it was), but not being able to bring her home went against all of our emotions. They put her under special lights, and she only had to stay one extra day. The day we went home was so exhilarating for us: packing up our belongings, hospital items, and our newborn baby girl.

Two years later, we were so excited to find out we were having another child. Like the first pregnancy Cher took care of herself, and took her pre-natal vitamins, staying away from caffeine and other medications.

Again, we wanted to be surprised of the gender of

this baby. Given the due date for the end of March, 1984, we again prepared, and knew we should look for another home, due to the small size of "Rachel's Room." At the time interest rates were 18%. Cher was looking in a giant real estate section of the paper one Sunday, and spotted a small 2 inch add for new twin homes being built in the Skippack area. The pre-construction interest rates were 9 ¼ %. As we drove out to see these homes, it was a very country-like feeling, and a wonderful area to raise a family. Entering the development and seeing the sample home, we knew it was a place we would like to be. Our little doll house in Glenside would be missed with so many special memories, but we could always come back to visit.

At 2:00 am on February 21, 1984, it was a snowy, wintry morning, when we were awakened. Not a dream this time, but Cher heard Rachel's call. She went to check on her, and as she reached to put her arms around her, she realized her water had broken. As the contractions started, she was puzzled because the due date was about 6 weeks later. We scrambled to get things together, along with Rachel, who needed to be dropped off at Oma's house.

When we arrived at the hospital, Cher again went into hard labor, but as soon as Sarah was born, there was something immediately wrong. Sarah was gasping for air, and doctors came from all directions. I was removed from the room, and instead of Sarah being placed into her mother's arms, she became the center of activity. Cher remembers thinking, "I just want to hold her," – this sweet, beautiful, tiny, little doll. "Sarah" which means "princess" or "to rule" was the name intended as a seal of the promise given to Abraham.

Questions immediately flooded our thoughts. What was happening? Why was this happening? Everything seemed okay, and we took all of the same pre-cautions as the first pregnancy. Is she going to be okay?

Cher was taken to another room, and doctors finally came in to tell us that Sarah has Hyaline Membrane Disease, being born pre-maturely her lungs were under developed and the surfactant was not present at this stage of development. From birth Sarah was using all of her life's strength to try to breathe. We then were told that she would be taken to another hospital, St. Christopher's in Philadelphia, in a special ambulance, in a bubble like incubator.

They let us know it was gravely serious. We asked what was the percentage of survival. They couldn't give us any hope. They also told us because she was on 80% oxygen to help her breathe, there could be other complications, if she survived.

Standing at Cher's bedside, after hearing this news, Cher began to cry, and the doctor's recommended that they bring Sarah into the room before they took her. At first, Cher being in shock, thought maybe it would be better just to remember how she looked when she was born. But she took the doctor's advice, and had them roll Sarah into the room next to where Cher was laying. She remembers reaching out to touch her little newborn pinky finger, knowing if she could only bring her home that she would be okay, and not knowing if this was the last time that she would see her alive. As Sarah's head was facing her, and she was looking into Cher's eyes, it was as if she knew this is my mom.

After they took Sarah away, I was standing at the foot of Cher's hospital bed. In the natural I would have begun to weep, however, I had one of those spiritual experiences that I will never forget, and it is still vivid in my memory to this day. Instead of falling apart, I felt physically the hand of God on my lower back, holding me up, and sustaining my emotions. I heard in my spirit the voice of the Lord say, "Be strong and of good courage."

That was all He said. I did not know whether to be strong and courageous, because if she died she would be with Him, or because she would be healed. This word, however, was so strong, and it carried us through this time of trial and testing.

During this same week of Sarah's birth, many loved ones were also hospitalized in different places. Cher was at Chestnut Hill Hospital, Sarah – St. Christopher's, Aunt Connie with a brain tumor at the Jefferson Hospital, and Virgie (my spiritual mom) in North Philadelphia.

Leaving Cher at the hospital, I went home to look up all of the scripture verses I could on breath. After just minutes, I set out to visit Sarah at St. Christopher's. It was heart-breaking to see your new born baby girl, only hours old, hooked up from head to toe with wires and breathing tubes. Laying my finger on hers, I prayed a prayer of faith believing that God would raise her up and heal her. I also quoted and declared boldly the promises of the healing verses of Scripture. Cher was in agreement with me from her hospital room. She would call the neonatal intensive care unit daily, believing that each day Sarah's strength and breathing would improve to eventually breathe on her own without the ventilator.

We knew this would be a testimony to our families on how we handled this trial.

> *"A righteous man may have many troubles, but the Lord delivers him from them all."*
>
> *– Psalm 34:19*

Cher came home from the hospital and began to visit Sarah with me daily. As Cher would hold her, talk to her, and feed her, again there was this feeling, "If I could bring you home, you would be okay!" Miraculously, after two weeks of neonatal intensive care, Sarah came home. What a day of rejoicing. Even now, it is not without tears, recognizing the wonderful works of God.

Cher came home.

Sarah came home.

Aunt Connie came home.

Virgie went home to be with the Lord!

> *"Jesus is the same yesterday, and today and forever." – Hebrews 13:8*

> *"For I am the Lord who heals you."*
> *– Ephesians 15:26*

He is Jehovah Rapha!

Regardless of your need, Romans 10:13 says: "Everyone who calls on the name of the Lord will be saved." (Healing and wholeness)

There is nothing impossible with God!

CHAPTER 11
GROWING YEARS

Proud Of Our Jewish Roots...

Rachel, being 2 ¾ yrs. older than Sarah, had a unique way of encouraging and loving her sister. Even today you can sense this special bond between the two of them that cannot be broken.

When it was time to send them to school, we wanted it to be a place that would reinforce what we were teaching them at home. They both attended a Christian Academy, which is located within the same church we came to know the Lord in. They learned His Word, academics, played sports, and also took piano lessons. Both girls were musically inclined. We wanted to encourage them enough to excel with the gifts the Lord had given them. So not to make it too much pressure with all of the other things they had going on, we alternated weeks of lessons, practicing in between; then, summers were off! We thank the Lord that they are still playing music, and are also a part of our worship band every week at Shalom!

As a young girl, Sarah had to wear glasses. We took her to an eye specialist at the Children's Hospital in Philadelphia. After years of examinations, and us praying, the doctor began to decrease her prescription for glasses. He did this each year, until she no longer needed any correction at all. To this day her eyesight is better than 20/20 vision. To God be the glory! As parents, once again, we were amazed at the goodness of God, to touch our daughter. We will never forget those days in the intensive care unit with weakened lungs, and now excelling in field hockey, basketball, and a singing voice from heaven that will send chills up and down your spine.

Rachel was also involved with basketball and field hockey. We remember traveling for both girls to their away games, and at home games standing on the side lines cheering them on. We wanted to support them, not embarrass them. We knew deep down that they were glad we were there.

Most people do not discover their life's calling or vocation at an early age, but Rachel did. As a little girl she expressed the desire to be a heart surgeon. We took her seriously, and over the years would purchase medical books, doctor's kits, heart models, etc. to help her learn. Her interest never faded. One night as a young adult, after coming home from a youth rally, she shared with us that during worship, the Lord spoke to her. The message was that her hands were going to be used. More on that later in this book.

During a season of prayer for my family's salvation, with a heart's desire to see them come to the Lord, I was impressed to have a Bat Mitzvah for Rachel. In a Jewish home it is customary when your daughter turns thirteen to have a ceremony that proclaims that the individual is a "Daughter of God's Commandment." We rented out a restaurant, invited family, friends, and church members to celebrate with us.

I wore my blue yarmulke with Jerusalem spelled on it, and blue and white tallis (prayer shawl), and led worship with instruments and singers. Due to the occasion, we limited the songs and message to Old Testament revelation. We had a Messianic Rabbi blow the Shofar, and carry the Torah throughout the crowd of people. Both Rachel and Sarah (3 years later) read scripture and said prayers in Hebrew and in English, just like I did when I was 13 and had my Bar Mitzvah (Son of God's Commandment). During both of these occasions, I took the opportunity to publicly bless and thank my parents for sending me to Sunday School and Hebrew School. I also quoted my Bar Mitzvah scripture reference from the book of Numbers that says God's desire is that all of His people would be prophets (Spokesman for Him).

> *"But Moses replied, Are you jealous for my sake? I wish that all the Lord's people were prophets and that the Lord would put His Spirit on them!"*
>
> *– Numbers 11:29*

Wondering what the people were experiencing during the service, we found out afterwards it was thoroughly enjoyed and well received. We know the Holy Spirit was there, and it was evident by what was said and the expressions upon the many faces there.

This is one of the traditions that we embraced for our daughters because of our Jewish heritage. We always wanted them to be proud of their Jewish roots, and remember the biblical significance in them. It's so easy in religion to be so busy with ceremony and ritual that God Himself can be left out. We never wanted this to happen in our lives.

CHAPTER 12
TRANSITION

God Showed His Faithfulness...

We watched as this little Assembly of God church grew from a handful of people to a few hundred. The people who attended became our family and close friends for eleven years.

As God blessed us with more growth, we moved from rental to rental, and stood by the Pastor through a church split. We lost many friends because even though there was some credence to their complaints, they went about it in the wrong way. This caused the Pastor to lose trust in people and became very insecure. As a result, the relationship between staff members became strained. After serving as the Assistant Pastor for almost two years and going through a building program which was now complete, there were not enough finances to support the staff.

Now in our new building, at our new location, the senior Pastor thought that the attendance would double within the first year. This did not happen. The Youth Pastor was laid off, and I assumed his responsibilities. When the church was being built every decision was made by faith anticipating instant growth, but still nothing financially changed. A board meeting was called with the decision already made that I also was to be laid off. I was told Friday would be my last day. I offered to get a part-time job to supplement a pay cut, until the finances were there. However, this was not considered. The board was not in agreement with the Pastor, but the decision was final. Since I was faithful to the Lord and the Pastor, this was very hurtful. We had invested so much of our lives here, and brought many people to the church. It would be very difficult for us to leave.

Knowing I had to support my family, I called one of my last places of employment, Cardone Industries, and miraculously dramatic changes in management were taking place at that time. The following Monday I started my new job in management/sales, and never missed a pay check.

Our calling and desire for ministry had not changed. Cher and I continued leading worship and ministry at the church without a position or title, while seeking God's direction. Knowing there were pastoral openings in our area, and close to our present church, we never considered them, because the previous Assistant Pastor split the church and drew people away. We wanted to prove that was not our intent. We wondered what God was doing, because our hearts simply wanted to serve Him.

God's answer was Romans 8:28: "And we know that in all things God works for the good of those who love

Him, who have been called according to His purpose."

As I continued in the sales job, we waited on the Lord for His perfect will, and did not put our names in to our district for possible openings. Some opportunities for ministry came to us, but we knew they were not where we were meant to be.

Just two months later, working at my desk, the President of the company where I worked invited the Pastors of our section to hold their meeting there. Out of all the buildings, and offices, the Presbyter of the southeast section of the Assemblies of God, walked right by my desk, and was surprised to see me there. He asked, "Why are you here?" I then told him the story, and he asked me if I would be interested in week-end ministry (Preaching part-time). There were a few families interested in starting a new church in the Bucks County area. He thought I would be a perfect fit for them. That Sunday I took my family and began to preach there. Each week we were invited back, and then on June 1, 1989 we formed a brand new home mission's congregation. Once again, God showed His faithfulness. When we didn't know what was going to happen; He did. When things were out of our hands, we were in His Hands.

I continued to work at my sales job. The demands of pioneering a new congregation, and working the full-time job which included flying from city to city at times, began to take its toll on my body. In the first year

I began having pains in my chest. I remember writing messages for Wednesday and Sundays on air flights between cities. After a visit to the emergency room, I was told I had chest wall syndrome, something I never heard of before. The walls surrounding my heart were irritated, and the doctor asked me "Are you under any stress?" My response was an emphatic "Yes!"

Our meetings were held on the second floor of a carpet warehouse in an industrial park. The conditions were not ideal (to say the least). To find the entrance of the building, you had to go to the dead end, drive around to the back of the building, pass the trash dumpster, and then walk up the flight of stairs. They had a triple net lease, which means we had to pay taxes and utilities in addition to the monthly rent. When we began, there was already a debt of thousands of dollars, and if that wasn't enough the largest family and their friends left shortly after we began.

Despite all of this, the presence and peace of God were evident, and we knew this was where the Lord was calling us.

One-by-one, the Lord was bringing those that were hurting, and we saw growth as we ministered to those that came our way. By faith we would always put out more chairs, expecting others to come. When we first had 20 in attendance, it literally brought tears to our eyes knowing God was at work. We have been blessed to see souls saved, and people sent out with the call of God in their lives. Within the first year the church expanded, building a sanctuary on the first floor, and we grew to over one hundred people.

> *"Being confident of this, that He who began a good work in you will carry it on to completion until the day of Christ Jesus." – Philippians 1:6*

God was with us not because of the "prime location" but because of the "peace" of God.

People would ask me as the Pastor, "What are we going to do?" "Are we going to buy land?" "Are we going to purchase a building?" At that time we survived week-to-week financially, and had no savings. By faith, without knowing the answer, I would say, "The Lord will provide." Multiple times, business men of financial means had promised us land, buildings, and finances all of which never panned out. However, each time a promise was made it gave us hope of what God was going to do.

After a few years, when zoning expired, we were informed that it would not be renewed.

Within a matter of weeks we had to be out. During our prayer time, a visiting pastor heard of our need for a facility. He told us about a building that we could possibly rent, not far from the Southampton area. About five miles away, in the Willow Grove area, the Free Methodist Church allowed us to meet early on Sunday mornings. We would have our service; then be out in time for their service to begin. As we started to grow here as a congregation, we were able to meet all the requirements, to become a sovereign Assembly of God church.

After a year and a half, we were notified by the Free Methodist Church, that we had thirty days to find another place. Again, now for the second time we possibly were facing extinction! We needed a place that was zoned and where there was ample parking. We were too small to afford a big facility, and too big to meet in a home. It was a Catch 22. We prayed about what direction to take. Cher had graduated from Phil-Mont Christian Academy, just a few miles away from where we were meeting. When Cher was in the 12th grade she was a 5th grade teacher's assistant, for one of her courses.

It just so happened that now this teacher was promoted to be the Principal of the Academy. We made an appointment to meet with her. As we shared our predicament with her, she thought it would be a great idea for the school to have a church using it on the week-ends. She gave us a green light, but the board gave us a red light. Days were running out, and she was going to meet with the board. She put in a good word for us, and after discussing it, and that we would take care of the place and pay $10,000 a year it was approved! God is always faithful, even if he brings us up until the last moments of the deadline! We were very thankful, and yet there was much work. We set up and tore down the chairs and furniture before and after every service for many years.

Think about it: First we met in a warehouse, then in a church building, then a gym. Regardless of where we met, or what the appearance was, God's Spirit was always present.

During these six and a half years of renting the school, we saw growth in numbers and the Spirit as well as experiencing waves of spiritual attacks. Families that appeared to be our greatest support became among those who split the church. One family, with the intent of starting their own church, began inviting our leaders to services in their home. At one Pastor's Christmas Banquet, each pastor was given the book "The Jezebel Spirit." I thought I knew all about that, so I put it on the top of a pile of books "to read." When we experienced this power struggle to take over control of the church, I read the book and it was word for word what we were going through. I also sought counsel on how to handle the situation, finding out that many pastors were going through the same thing. King Ahab handed his authority to his wife Jezebel when he was supposed to rule. As the Pastor and spiritual leader of the congregation it was my responsibility to confront the attack; and I did.

In the beginning of 1998, the Lord gave me a scripture that I spoke by faith for all to hear. It was II Samuel 7:10: "God said I will provide a place for my people, and will plant them, so they will have a home of their own." In the fall of 1998 I felt the Lord impress me to call the church to pray specifically for a building, and that God was going to do a quick work.

Also, to add a time of fasting, asking God to reveal to us His direction. The NEXT Day, I received a call from Cher's brother, who is a realtor. He began to tell me that the Free Methodist Church that we had rented years ago was now for sale. That night Cher and I met with the board at the church property, and prayed. Within 24 hours we submitted an agreement of sale. After bidding above asking price, the acceptance signature was supposed to be returned within three days, but we did not receive it. Again there was spiritual hindrance, interfering with our blessing. It was a very unsettling feeling. Was someone else over bidding us? Was someone behind the scenes trying to stop what God was doing? Finally, the signed contract came through. Blessed be the Name of the Lord!

Our settlement date was December 18, 1998, the same year that God's prophetic Word was spoken by faith. One week later, the LAST Sunday of the month, of the same year, we had our first service! It was a time of dancing and celebration. We also testified of the faithfulness of our God!

> *"No weapon forged against you will prevail, and you will refute every tongue that accuses you. This is the heritage of the servants of the Lord,*

and this is their vindication from me, declares the Lord." – Isaiah 54:17

Truly God has proven Himself faithful!!

We never told anyone, but when we were renting this church building in the early 90's, Cher, the girls, and I did a Jericho march in the snow, surrounding the entire property, believing that God would grant this to our congregation.

Our vision has always been to be a multi-cultural congregation, breaking down walls that divide, and providing a place where God is worshipped in Spirit and in truth, "Where the Peace of God Reigns." This is why we named the church Shalom, because of God's faithfulness and He promises to give us "peace."

CHAPTER 13
OPEN DOORS

God Always Goes Beyond Our Expectations ...

Along with our church ministry, the Lord has opened up other doors over the years. Seemingly out of nowhere I was contacted by the President of the National Religious Broadcasters Association, who was also the media spokesman for Evangelist Billy Graham.

He took Cher and me out to lunch and suggested that we begin a one minute devotion on Philadelphia's largest Christian Radio station WZZD/WFIL. I began weekly going to the station to tape the devotion, and called it "A Moment of Peace." It opened with Cher singing her original song, "Piece by Piece." Later on a fifteen minute spot became available, and we produced portions of our worship and preaching from the Sunday morning service.

The prophecies that we had personally received from different evangelists, "that we would reach multitudes", were now literally being fulfilled. After being on the radio for a few years, people in the tri-state area that we would bump into would recognize my voice, and tell us that they were encouraged. With this burning desire to reach many with the Gospel, we purchased a number of television commercials, aired on secular channels such as USA, TNT, and CNN. Along with good reports, we also received some death threats from Jewish people who did not like the idea of mixing Judaism with Christianity.

However, this was not our idea. It's God's. All of Christianity has its roots in Judaism. The Old Testament prophets foretold where the Messiah would be born, how He would die, that He would be rejected by His own, and that He would conquer death. We just proclaimed these truths. We also appeared on the local television, Trinity Broadcast Network, sharing our music and testimony on the Praise the Lord Show – hosted by our dear friend Kim Sledge Allen, as well as other television ministry invitations.

We began the Hourglass Ministries as an evangelistic outreach of Shalom. After Cher received a vision of an "Hourglass," she knew it was for the time that we are now living.

> *"So you also must be ready, because the Son of Man will come at an HOUR when you do not expect Him." – Matthew 24:44*

It was given to her after a traumatic family fire, and the Lord revealed that the return of Jesus is near, and the enemy knows his time is running out.

"The thief comes only to steal, and kill, and destroy, I have come that they may have life, and have it to the full." – John 10:10

"Greater is He that is in you, than he that is in the world." – I John 4:4

Hourglass ministries have included coffee houses, concerts, evangelistic outreaches, and Bible studies.

God always goes beyond our expectations in bringing blessing and opening doors.

When we would go to Ocean City on the Jersey shore, on vacation with Rachel and Sarah, there were times that we would take them to the place where we met on that sunny day as teenagers in Longport. Over the years, the motel was converted to one room condominiums, available to purchase. Because of the sentimental value, we thought many times how nice it would be, to buy one, but the price was prohibitive. A few years ago, when the real estate market dropped, prices were reduced, we made a low offer that was accepted. We felt so blessed that the Lord would open this door for us, for a place of retreat, and come to find out that He was planning something more.

When we met at the abstract company for settlement, usually papers are signed, keys are exchanged, and good-bye. As we were waiting for the seller's arrival, we introduced ourselves to the seller's broker, Linda, who usually does not attend these settlements. She felt she wanted to be here on this day. After a little while the seller and sales agent Kathleen arrived, but we still did not get to the business at hand – the real estate transaction.

Linda was apologizing for her phone calls, and Cher said we understand, being in the ministry how busy it can get. We could see questions arising in their minds as they started asking how does the name Goldbloom, which is a Jewish name, and being a Pastor, go together. This opened up for us to share our story of where we met, and how we came to know the Lord. The conversation continued and the three ladies all asked for a Shalom card. Since the seller came from out of state, they were taking her to dinner after settlement, and they invited us to come.

During this time, Cher and I looked at each other, knowing God was doing something beyond the purchase of this condo. After the business was finished, we continued this conversation out into the lobby, and then down the stairs, going outside of the building in Ocean City, New Jersey. As we were standing on the sidewalk, Kathleen said, "If your church was here, we would come." God was birthing something in our hearts, and we knew it. Linda had gone ahead to the restaurant, by the way which is named Manna, (Bread from Heaven). She called to see where everyone was. We accepted the invitation to join them. We knew our church was too far for them to attend on a regular basis, (two hours away), but we mentioned we could bring a

Bible Study to them, recognizing their spiritual hunger. Towards the end of the meal, Cher asked Linda if we could use a room in her office for the Bible Study. Linda answered immediately, "NO! You can use my home!" We will never forget that supernatural moment. We all felt it, and were so excited about our paths crossing.

Our first Bible Study was Sunday evening, June 1, 2008. We brought our guitars for worship, and began a study on the reliability of the Scriptures. After each study there is time for questions and answers, with a meal following. We know it is not a coincidence that the place where we met, also became a place of ministry, on the same day we started the church! This ministry still continues, and is bearing much fruit.

On Shalom's 15th Year Anniversary we invited our friend and Bishop Herb Hutchinson to be our guest speaker. The following year, for his church's anniversary (Center of Unbroken Praise) Egg Harbor, New Jersey, our worship team was invited to lead worship for their special service. They had an evangelist who came from the Navajo Indian reservation in Arizona to preach. As we led worship, the anointing of the Spirit was very strong, and energized the spiritual atmosphere for the preaching of God's Word. When he began to speak, you could sense humility in his personality for such a passionate speaker.

When his message was concluded, he began to prophesy to different people, including a personal message to our daughter Sarah, which she received with tears. Spontaneously, the congregation approached the stage to financially bless this evangelist. Now that the service was over, the evangelist walked directly to me, with something in his closed fist that he wanted to give to me. I certainly did not want to take money from this humble man, but when he opened his hand he gave me a ring with an eagle on it and said, "Soar with the eagle."

We had never met or spoken before this, and he had no idea of the struggles we were going through in ministry. Ever since that day, seven years ago, I wear this ring when I preach, and it reminds me to "Soar with the eagle."

> *"But those who hope in the Lord will renew their strength. They will soar on wings like eagles; they will run and not grow weary, they will walk and not be faint." – Isaiah 40:31*

We have even named our motorcycle ministry, "Eagle's Wings," because of this scripture.

> *"Now to Him who is able to do immeasurably more than all we ask or imagine, according to His power that is at work within us, to Him be glory in the church and in Messiah Jesus throughout all generations, for ever and ever amen."*
> *– Ephesians 3:20-21*

CHAPTER 14

Angels, Visions and Spiritual Dreams

There have been times when we believe we have been visited by angels in human form, to help us in our time of need. Whether it was for physical protection, a word of encouragement, or to be given a blessing, we are in awe of our heavenly Father's goodness to us.

> *"Do not forget to entertain strangers, for by doing so some people have entertained angels without knowing it." – Hebrews 13:2*

Like the vision of the Hourglass, and the ministries that have followed to confirm it, we have experienced dreams from the Lord that also have encouraged us on this journey.

One night Cher had a dream, and when she woke up she shared it with me. She said it felt like a spiritual dream from God. In it she saw the stage and fellowship hall where we were seated with Pastor Joe Van Koevering from "God's News Behind the News." We had never met him before, but had watched his television show for years ... which made her wonder – What did this mean?

We have always enjoyed going to Florida on vacation, but had never been to the St. Petersburg area where Pastor Joe's church is located. After starting our Bible study at Linda's home, she invited us to stay at her Florida home for vacation. It was located in Sarasota, Florida. While we were there, about a year after Cher's dream, we decided to visit Pastor Joe's church for a Wednesday Night Bible study. I had called to find out the time of the service weeks earlier. Since it began at 7:00 PM, we arrived at 6:30, but there was no one in the sanctuary. We heard voices coming from another wing of the church. A lady approached us and asked if she could help us. We told her we were looking for the Bible study, and she explained that it was cancelled, and they were having a Passover Seder and dinner by reservation. At first we were disappointed thinking we had to leave.

Cher said to this woman, "Oh we are from out of town, and my husband is a Jewish Pastor." She motioned to us to wait, and left for a minute. She returned asking us to follow her through the side entrance, entering the fellowship hall. She pointed to the only two empty seats, and told us to sit there. As we walked to our table, with many people in attendance, there was a Messianic Rabbi speaking. Approaching our seats we realized we were being directed to sit with Pastor Joe and his wife. The presence of the Lord was overwhelming as we knew this was the place in fulfillment of Cher's dream.

The Seder had already been in progress, so we did not want to introduce ourselves. When it was time for the meal, we had the opportunity to greet Pastor Joe.

He immediately said, "I've met you before," and he was very kind and made us feel welcomed. We knew it was our first time meeting him, and again he exclaimed, "I know I've met you before!" "Maybe in a dream." We knew God had brought our paths together, and as we shared, there were many common experiences, in ministry and our personal lives. We did not share the "dream" with him at this time because we had just met, and wanted to wait for the right time.

At the end of the Seder, the Rabbi pointed to a table that had books and tracts he had written. I whispered to Cher, saying we know the man that wrote one of the tracts he had mentioned, and realized then, who the speaker was. Thirty-one years earlier, we met with his mother, Marianne Fischer, a Jewish believer and Holocaust survivor, who was a photographer. We were planning for her to do our wedding pictures, and while making plans, her son John walked in, and she introduced us to him. This was in Willow Grove, Pennsylvania, and the last time we had seen him, until this night. After the Seder, we introduced ourselves, and Rabbi John Fischer told us that when we walked in, we looked familiar.

The Lord was letting us know and reminding us, that He was continuing to direct our steps.

At the end of the evening Pastor Joe gave us his information, and asked us to stay in touch, to see what God is doing!

The following year we attended our first International Prophecy Conference at his church. In between sessions, Pastor Joe made time for us to have lunch together. At that time, we shared Cher's "dream" with him, and he re-called the words he had said: "Maybe we met in a dream." It was an exciting moment knowing the Lord had brought us together. We also had a time of friendship, and expressed anticipation of what God is doing.

Over the years, many have said that we should write a testimonial book, which after this conference was birthed! While we waited at the airport to return to Philadelphia, we wrote the outline for this book.

The next year at the International Prophecy Conference, Pastor Joe introduced us to Bob Armstrong, an ordained minister and editor of various publications; another one of God's supernatural appointments. As we spoke we realized we had a lot in common, and knew some of the same people. There was an instant connection, and we spoke of our story that we were in the process of writing. That day we had lunch with him and Pastor Joe, and continued our conversation. Bob gave us his card, and said we could contact him for friendship, and help concerning the book. God certainly was doing something in our midst!

CHAPTER 15
PRESENT DAY

Shalom...

Cher and I continue serving the Lord at Shalom Assembly of God and wherever the Lord opens up the door for us. The last few months we have gone through a season of grieving at the loss of my mom, after suffering with COPD, and lung cancer. During this time we had the opportunity to share about eternity with her. While in the emergency room she expressed to us of a prayer that she does pray. "Even though it is not a Jewish prayer," mom said, "Now I lay me down to sleep, I pray the Lord my soul to keep, and if I die before I wake, I pray the Lord my soul to take." This was the first time she ever verbally mentioned anything of a personal prayer time in her life.

Also, at the end of conversations she would say "Send my love", but after the hospital visit, as we were leaving Cher said, "I love you", and back to us she replied, "I love you." We know the Lord was softening her heart. The last two days of her life she was in a sleep state. On the Wednesday evening before she died, at our prayer meeting, there was an urgency in prayer for mom's eyes to be open to receive her Messiah. The next morning while in prayer, Cher's mom (Shirley) asked the Lord to reveal Himself to my mom (Irene). In Shirley's spirit He said, "I did." In His Words he said, "Irene." "It is Me."

As my mom's physical condition was deteriorating we planned a lunch and time to discuss final arrangements. Sitting at my parent's dining room table, with Cher, my sister's Amy and Jennifer, and my dad, Eugene, my mom asked me to do her funeral service to be held at a Jewish Cemetery where her parents (my grand-parents) are buried. What an honor and privilege to be able to do this for her, and she seemed very content in leaving the details in my hands. It turned out to be a beautiful day for a grave-side service. There were many family members, friends, and people from Shalom that came to support us and to remember mom.

"Rachel's Dream" – Our daughter Rachel phoned us one evening, to share this dream. She is very careful to express that something is "a word from the Lord" or "a dream", and yet she knew this was the real thing. In the dream Rachel was handed a letter that was written by mom-mom (my mother). This letter had been intentionally written and put aside, and Rachel was not supposed to have it until mom-mom died. The color of the card was cream, and it had hand-painted flowers on it that were mostly blue and red with green leaves. The writing was in mom-mom's cursive writing, and saying nice/happy things. It was signed "Love, mom-mom," and under her name she wrote Hebrews 11:1-44.

In the dream Rachel recognized that this is the chapter on Faith, and felt this was mom-mom's way of saying she believed. Cher and Oma were also a part of this dream, and by the reactions on their faces, Rachel knew they were all thinking the same thing.

As Rachel looked up the verses in her Bible, she realized Hebrews did not have 44 verses, but if you continue reading it speaks that we are "surrounded by a cloud of witnesses" and encourages us to run the race marked out for us. The conclusion that Rachel came to was to compare the people in the faith chapter to dad. The theme of the chapter being Old Testament men and women who had been promised certain things, but never actually saw those things come to pass or be fulfilled in their lifetime. Yet they remained faithful and consistent, and because of their faithfulness, the promises were fulfilled. Rachel says she related this to me, and just because I never heard it out of mom's mouth, does not mean she did not believe.

This past Father's Day, June 19th 2011, which was also my birthday, by Cher's invitation, my dad came to Shalom's worship service. It was wonderful seeing him in the house of the Lord, sitting with his grand-children. What a beautiful birthday present. He knows he has a seat waiting for him whenever he comes to join us.

Cher's mom continues to serve the Lord at Shalom, and is a blessing to us with her continued love, support and encouragement. She serves on our deacon board, and teaches our "Women of Honor Devotion." She has been a Godly example to her family, and to those around her.

Cher's dad, Joe, is now retired and is keeping very busy serving the Lord at his church. He just celebrated his 75 birthday with his kids, grand-kids, and great grand-kids. We are a blessed family and it continues to grow!

We just celebrated Rachel's 30th birthday, with her husband Ben, (who is continuing his studies in the medical field) and their daughter, Charlotte. Charlotte Love is the "Joy of our hearts." She turned two in February. Ben and Rachel are expecting their second child in December, and we just found out they are having another girl!!

Rachel graduated with her Master's Degree as a Physician's Assistant at the Philadelphia University. She is currently on the open heart surgery team at a hospital in Philadelphia. She also continues to play the piano on our worship team. God fulfilled His promise to her, where she is "using her hands", touching hearts in worship with her melodic style, and touching hearts "literally" in surgery.

Sarah, now 27, graduated with a degree in Psychology at the Eastern University.

She is an assistant to the lieutenants and Chief at our local police department, and heads up victims services for the township. Sarah also is a singer/songwriter with a style of her own, and a voice that is soulful and convicting. Where her lungs were once weak, the Lord's healing touch has given her a powerful unique singing ability. She has also been gifted in playing many musical instruments. Once her eye sight was poor, now better than 20/20, not just physically, but she is able to see into the hearts of those hurting and needing compassion.

Sarah's Song: "Eyes of Grace" ... And you look at me with eyes of grace, You said I love you no matter what you've done. Just as I am. You love me, just as I am.

It's the peace that flows like a river...the joy that I've received...can only come from the maker...who's paid the price for you and me.

As a family we have it covered: Mind (Sarah with her psychology degree), Body (Rachel and Ben with their medical careers) and Soul (Cher and Myself), all to the glory of God!!

A Completed Jew ...
Through The Messiah

The offer Jesus (Yeshua) extends of everlasting life and peace are available to people of every race, and religious background.

> *Jesus said, "Come to me, all you who are weary and burdened, and I will give you rest."*
> *– Matthew 11:28*

> *"For He Himself is our peace, who has made Jew and Gentile one, and has destroyed the barrier, the dividing wall of hostility." – Ephesians 2:14*

In the Messiah, there is no longer division between classes, tribes, or colors.

When you repent of your sins, and invite Jesus into your life, you receive forgiveness of sins, the assurance of eternal life and your name is written in the "Lamb's Book of Life."

> *"You are all sons of God through faith in Messiah Jesus." – Galatians 3:26*

> *"There is neither Jew nor Greek, slave nor free, male nor female, for you are all one in Messiah Jesus." – Galatians 3:28*

We have discovered that believing and applying the promises of scripture have become the recipe for victory in our lives. We start each day with a de-caff Dunkin Donuts coffee, as we read our Daily Devotion, and have a time of prayer. When you read the history of the people of Israel in the scriptures, those who were blessed centered their lives around the worship of God and obedience to His commands. We encourage you to find a Bible proclaiming, Jesus exalting, congregation that makes room for the moving of the Holy Spirit, so that you can be encouraged in your faith.

The Apostle Peter said not to think something is wrong, after you come to the Lord and you experience problems, trials, and fiery temptations. For this is the normal walk for every believer. In Ephesians 6 we are reminded that we are all in a spiritual battle and must daily clothe ourselves with the full armor of God that he has provided. This is how you will be victorious in your walk with the Lord.

> *"You will keep in perfect peace him whose mind is steadfast, because he trusts in You."*
>
> *– Isaiah 26:3*

> *"Do not be anxious about anything, but in everything, by prayer and petition, with thanksgiving, present your requests to God. And the peace of God, which transcends all understanding, will guard your hearts and your minds in Messiah Jesus." – Philippians 4:6-7*

We have found that the peace and presence of God, regardless of circumstances is with us, when we keep our eyes focused on Him. During seasons of testing and trials, we have learned not to lean on man for the answers, but to trust God in our times of weakness; and He will once again prove Himself faithful.

In each step of our journey, in followings God's will for our lives, there has been attack and opposition. Nothing has been easy, but we rejoice in every small victory, recognizing God's power and plan is at work and will prevail. So when you find yourself in similar situations, keep your focus on Him, and allow the Lord to guide your path and you too will find "Where the Peace of God Reigns."

As you have read our story, we trust your faith has been strengthened.

If you are one who would like to receive the Messiah Jesus into your life, please pray the following prayer:

Jesus, I know that I have done things that are wrong, and have not been all that God intended me to be. I believe you lived on earth, died for my sins to make me clean and rose again so that I may live forever as part of God's family. I ask for forgiveness for these wrongs, and ask that you make me whole again. Please come into my life, and change me, and help me live my life for you. I surrender all that my life has been, and my life as it will be in the future. In Jesus' name. Amen

If you have said this prayer, please contact us to let us know. Our web-site is shalomag.com. We would love to rejoice with you!

It is important that you know you are now one of God's children. Tell others about your new life in Jesus, read your Bible every day, and find a church of believers that can help you grow in your walk with the Lord.

> *"The Lord bless you and keep you; the Lord make His face shine upon you and be gracious to you; the Lord turn His face towards you and give you peace." – Numbers 6:24-26*

If you are ever in the Willow Grove area of Pennsylvania (just north of Philadelphia) we would love to have you as our guest!

Shalom Assembly of God
1862 Kimball Avenue
Willow Grove, PA 19090

Sunday Service:
10:00 AM
Wednesday School of the Spirit
7:00 PM

www.shalomag.com